REAL MEDICINE

ALTERNATIVE

HOCKEY

(IF ONLY THIS STETHOSCOPE COULD TALK)

Tellwell Talent
www.tellwell.ca

ISBN
978-1-77370-020-5 (Hardcover)
978-1-77370-019-9 (Paperback)
978-1-77370-021-2 (eBook)

Dedicated to my family, my "teachers", my teammates, my colleagues, my patients and especially my wife Elaine Warren-Blais whom have given me the inspiration to write about the journey and experiences we took together over the years.

CONTENTS

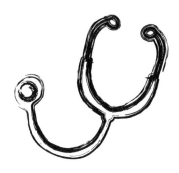

VOLUME II
MEMOIRS OF A CANADIAN HOCKEY DOCTOR
(MEDICINE BY DAY, HOCKEY BY NIGHT)

CHAPTER 1
MEDICINE BY DAY, HOCKEY BY NIGHT. 61

CHAPTER 2
TEACHING THE NEXT GENERATION
AND THE EVOLUTION OF FAMILY MEDICINE 109

CHAPTER 3
TALES FROM THE OFFICE -
SOME AMAZING OR NOT 145

PREFACE

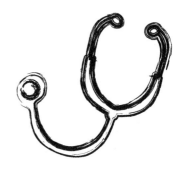

When I was thinking about a title for my book, I had two titles in mind: *Real Medicine, Alternative Hockey* and *If Only This Stethoscope Could Talk*. *Real Medicine, Alternative Hockey* would nicely tie the two volumes of my book together since the stories and writings were about real medicine and alternative hockey, both of my loves. Then the other title, *If Only This Stethoscope Could Talk*, relates to the insight you get from the "sacred" interaction that occurs between the family physician and his patient. I will let you decide what you think the best title for the book should be.

If only this stethoscope could talk …

As it hang around my neck, it would tell stories about my encounters with my patients and their families, both in humorous and serious times. They gave me the privilege to care for them and aid them medically, psychologically and sometimes spiritually. As the stethoscope touched their chests, it cemented the doctor-patient relationship with them, which has lasted many years, some spanning four family generations (true family medicine).

The stethoscope would have listened as I taught the medical students and family medicine residents over the years in my office or in the hospitals. I would relate to them "What Medical School Didn't Prepare You For (But Your Future Depends Upon)" as I introduced them to medical practice management in addition to the other medical topics that Osler and Hippocrates had taught to their students. As well the stethoscope would have been with me on my travels to attend my continuing medical education conferences throughout the world, and it would know how I loved to write about them.

In addition my stethoscope would be able to tell stories of my love for hockey and how some of my writings tied them to my practice of family medicine.

If only this stethoscope could talk, it would document my journey from a medical student and family medicine resident in the late 1970s and early 1980s into the family physician I am today, who has practised family medicine for over thirty years, beginning in the late 20th century and leading into the 21st century.

If only this stethoscope that hangs around my neck could talk, it would note the discoveries of new medical conditions/illnesses and the new revolutionary medications and treatments for them. As we progressed into the 21st century we could have never dreamed of such possibilities in the 20th century. It would talk about the change in medicine from a paternalistic/doctor all-knowing/illness centred concept to a more holistic and patient centred family medicine approach. Patients started to take control and ownership of their health and wellness. This was ushered in by technical changes such as the internet in the late 20th century, where there was easier access to medical information. Where would there not be a little humour in the fact that with the computer and EMR (Electronic Medical Record) that you did not need to have bad handwriting to get into medical school. In addition pharmacists no longer have to take the handwriting interpretation course, as it has now been removed from the pharmacy curriculum because doctors now type their prescriptions. Now only if you could decipher the signature of which doctor sent it.

In the two-volume book I have endeavoured to relate my encounters between that stethoscope and the patients it touched and my journey as a family physician. Over my career as a family physician I have recorded my thoughts and my writings and compiled them into these two volumes. Volume one is titled *The Medicine Man* and includes stories that I wrote about my first ten years in family medicine practice between 1983 and 1993. This was the time in family medicine when medicine moved from much simpler times into the next phase of the brave new medical world. Next there is volume two - Memoirs of a Canadian Hockey Doctor (Medicine by Day, Hockey by Night). Here as a family physician in the early 21st century (2001 to 2017), I write about my adventures in travel and medicine. Also included are some previously published articles for publications such as *Stitches* (humour magazine) and the *Canadian Family Physician* as well as some unpublished articles. I continued

Dr.Guy R.Blais sitting in the replica Montreal Canadiens'
dressing room in front of Ken Dryden's stall at the
Hockey Hall of Fame in Toronto, Ontario.

to write about my love of hockey and how it was tied into my family medicine career, thus the title for volume two. During this time and even today the world continues to proceed at lightning speed through the introduction of social media and the electronic medical chart affecting how medicine is practised and will be practised in the future.

So hopefully my stethoscope will have a chance to talk and continue to be a symbol of the doctor. Presently it is threatened by new technology and with the introduction of ultrasound/echocardiogram machines in many clinics. If it leaves us, lost will be the art of listening to your patient's heart. Sometimes you need to try and slow things down and listen with your stethoscope and let it talk and hear the "heart" of the patient's stories. It will help you to develop that doctor-patient relationship.

So through my writings I have given you a chance to slow things down by reading about a family physician and his stethoscope/goalie stick. You can see how a family physician can still love his career/vocational choice after all these years and still see the wonder of it as well. In addition how I can use my writing as an outlet to express myself in this new brave world. I hope this book of my stories and tales will give you much enjoyment and provide you insight into a family medicine career through listening to what would have been heard "if only this stethoscope could talk." The other title, *Real Medicine/Alternative Hockey* may sum up my writings. Let me know what you think but more importantly enjoy this book.

VOLUME I
THE MEDICINE MAN
BY DR. GUY BLAIS, MD, CCFP

Anecdotes of Family Medicine:
MY FIRST TEN YEARS

INTRODUCTION

Many people dream of writing a book. There is a romantic feeling generated when one thinks of becoming an author. Some people write to become famous and others just want to see their ideas and feelings put down on paper. They do that so that others may enjoy their writings whether it is humorous or soul seeking. The latter is the reason I wrote this collection of happy and sad stories, which are always thought provoking in some manner.

I am a doctor, and it is my life. No matter how hard I tried to write about other topics or use other styles of literary work, I failed. However, when I wrote from my heart and my experiences, the words came more easily. I hope you will feel the energy and the enthusiasm in my writing.

Medicine and its field have changed in many ways since I first entered medical school in the late 1970s. As many of my colleagues and fellow doctors did, we entered with dreams and our wish was to save and help mankind. Throughout the gruelling years of training, internship and long hours of looking after our fellow man, these may become tarnished. However, what keeps me going and helps me get through the trials and tribulations is the humour of my patients and friends. Laughter is the best medicine. Therefore I hope by relating some of my stories, they will bring some "health" to your life.

This collection of stories is from the first ten years of my practice. They are mostly humorous and lighthearted, followed by the last two entries, which are more expressive of how medicine affects the doctor from being on the outside, and later on the inside, looking out at its effects. For I am a medicine man and life is a special journey with the spirits in which you believe.

CHAPTER 1
THE EARLY YEARS

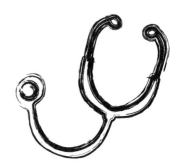

From our early years, we all believed doctors were like deity, and this is the ideal we would like to attain so that we can heal people. Well, this idea got tarnished quickly. It all started with my medical examination for admission to medical school. All doctors are supposed to have a bedside manner like Marcus Welby, speaking in a grandfatherly voice and knowing all. Picture yourself as a young male patient going to a doctor for a check-up and waiting for him to enter the room. In strides a tall, skinny, forty-year-old English gentleman who promptly examines me without uttering a word. The last thing he says is, "Drop your pants and cough." I was ready to laugh as I remembered a scene from an old army movie of soldiers lined up for their physicals undergoing the same routine.

The doctor was gone before I finished coughing and out the door without saying whether I was healthy or not or even goodbye. I was only to find out later that he was my neuroanatomy professor, and he was not used to talking to live people.

Well, I made it through the medical and the interview. Many a doctor will tell you the one day that stands out in their mind is the first day of anatomy. You know, the day you get to see your cadaver. We all wondered how we would react. I envisioned a scene out of a horror movie as people are running through a cold, dark, morgue-like room. As young doctors-to-be, we are supposed to get used to it. We eventually do. I found later I enjoyed anatomy, but I remember relating my enthusiasm to other friends in the university at lunchtime. As I described vividly the excitement of dissection in the laboratory, my friends turned green and were on the verge of fainting. I could not understand why they didn't appreciate the beauty of the body. I guess lunch was not the right time to talk about the dissection!

Everybody remembers a classmate who stands out for one thing or another. I had a friend who was a great artist (a Fred Netter to be), who loved to draw caricatures of his classmates. One day in class, while a professor was lecturing on a huge sliding blackboard, he noticed that he was running out of room. He pulled up the blackboard and to everybody's surprise there was a huge drawing of our classmate, who was six feel fall and looked like a giant. The artist, however, made a few adjustments, including a bolt on each side of the neck and a flat top head and presto, our unknowing classmate was now Frankenstein's monster. The huge lecture hall was filled with laughter. Dr. Frankenstein wished he could have slipped out, but he always sat in the front row. The professor glared at him as though it was his fault.

The story was not over. One day on a university hospital ward (on obstetrics many years later), nurses were heard yelling and laughing uncontrollably, "It's him, it's him!" My friend Dr. F couldn't understand why he was so popular. He was just up there to do a consult. He knew he was important, but this was ridiculous. There pinned to a corkboard was a head view of him in his famous pose as Frankenstein's monster, complete with the flat top haircut and bolts in the neck. It had been left behind as a legacy to Dr. F, and the nurses did not realize until that day that he actually existed. The nurses would never let him forget this until this day.

Medical school is a tough four years or so. Anybody who knew us when we were students knew things could get quite crazy, and we had just the way of letting the pressure off.

In late January every year, we as medical students would put on a medical show. To the general public it may have seemed crude. Some of the skits were excellent. Some of the highlights included the Cretin Choir dressed in greens and with our faces painted as corpses. We were well directed by a zombie. As a choir we sang in monotone voices, renditions of "I am bloated, I am passing no gas," "Horny," and later on, a new song was written called "Leprosy," sung to the tune of "Yesterday" - "Leprosy, I am only half the man I used to be."

We also used to make fun of the engineers and especially the dentists. I went through medical school during the disco craze. I had a classmate who dressed up as a dancing dentist with a huge toothbrush, and he danced to a disco tune. He would talk with a lisp, moving a toothbrush like nobody had seen. His first appearance was in the "Wizard of Obs" as the dentist without a brain - "If Only I Had a Brain." Each year he was written into the medical show to give an encore, gyrating with the giant brush like John Travolta.

Talking about the disco era, strobe lights were a popular thing at parties. As a medical student I was at a post-obstetrics rotation party, and one of my classmates grabbed two pieces of pizza with two forks, and as he was bringing it up to his mouth, they dropped in front of the strobe lights and appeared to be falling in slow motion onto his lap. What a mess!

Sometimes we took our studying too far. Like the time we took my friend's skeleton, wearing a cowboy hat, in a truck with us on a car race in the fall. There were quite a few stares when we stopped for gas. This didn't bother us, and we just kept driving with Dr. Bones.

The Diligent Doctor

Many people think that doctors are born conscientious. Or is this trait developed in medical school? If only the public really knew the truth. When I was a medical student on my medical rotation, I was unusually put in a group with six female medical students at a downtown hospital. Every afternoon at about 2 or 3 p.m., one of our young aspiring conscientious female medical students would disappear into the bowels of the Metropolitan Hospital, nowhere to be found. She would not answer her pages. We wondered what duties for the good of mankind she was performing. One day one of my fellow students stumbled upon her in the Y wing watching one of the popular "while the stomach turns" soap operas. This is what she had been doing every afternoon. Her addiction and her idea of diligence were discovered to the disdain of us all.

We also had a female, Dr. Demarcos, who would say she was off to see her sick grandmother and have us cover as she shopped for shoes downtown.

My classmate also related a story to me about one of our classmates who was with him on a surgery rotation as a student. As part of our duties, if asked, we would start an intravenous on surgery patients. Bashfully, one of the students came up to my classmate and asked if he could start an IV for him because he hadn't started one yet (this was the last day). My friend looked at him and said, "How come you didn't learn or try by now?" He said he didn't need to know because he was going to be a "Valium doctor" (psychiatrist). Since this was the last day of the rotation, my friend just did it for him. Later, we learned that this same medical student was running a plant rental business out of his home while going to medical school. If you called him, you would get an answering machine stating he was "JM Plant Rental Services." This was confirmed by other colleagues of mine, who knew him better. Oh yeah, he did become a psychiatrist in sunny California.

I will tell you the last story before you start believing how unconscientiously and untrustworthy our medical profession is. One of my colleagues, a very pleasant lad, had a tendency to party and cause disturbances at various locations, including the residence on campus where he was residing. He was known for his cunning recipes of making cold mushroom soup and adding ice cream to it and cooking it as you would a rare steak and then eating it from the pot with a ladle as we all got to look on. This is mild compared to some of his antics at restaurants, antics that were straight out of "Animal House."

He led a double life, plotting his every move with diligence and precision. First, he became our sports representative. He then did a medical summer project and later became our class president, and then finally he ran for University Council and won. Being trusting and naïve young individuals, we thought it was all done because he was interested in and enjoyed these activities. Later on we discovered he had applied to become a Rhodes Scholar and won a scholarship. His friends later told us that each move was a political one and had paid off despite his well-known and less savoury side. So off to Oxford he went. He eventually came back and finished his medical degree, only to take a law degree. The Rhodes Scholar then moved to the west coast of Canada and practised litigation law. But guess for whom!

Really, we aren't all like that! Truthfully swear to Osler! We matured and became interns.

Code III and the Devil's Grip

There are many stories I could share with you that would restore your faith in the medical profession, but I don't want to bore you, so I will only tell you the interesting ones, no matter how awful they are.

When I was an intern on Pediatrics, late on a Friday afternoon (note it was not Wednesday and I was still there and not golfing) a sick five-year-old boy with a high fever and a bad cough came on the ward. I began examining him closely, not wanting to miss anything. I examined him all too closely, as he promptly coughed all over my face with the contents of his respiratory secretions, which I promptly wiped from my face. I politely finished the examination and found he had a throat infection, which probably stemmed from a viral cause.

I was off that weekend resting up to start my medical rotation. On Sunday morning I woke up with the most severe right chest pain, which worsened as the day went on. If I took a deep breath, I was in agony. My wife said I should see a doctor, but doctors don't like to see other doctors because we see enough of them every day. Also after what I told you about our medical student days, you wouldn't blame me. But she dragged me to an emergency department, and the doctor diagnosed me with pleurisy. I went home and started my medical rotation the next day, not missing a day because we all are very stoic or stupid. That morning I was talking to an obstetrics resident who previously had been a general practitioner before deciding to deliver babies for a living. He listened to my story and promptly said I had Devil's Grip. I said, "What is that"? He said it was caused by a virus, and young adults don't get the same symptoms as children, but get a pleurisy-like condition that is severe. So being diligent, I went and read about it. It is caused by the Coxsackie virus, and in retrospect this is what the child had. What a way to make a diagnosis with me as the guinea pig!

The story is not over. Of all days, some unfortunate patient had a cardiac arrest on the ninth floor that day. Code III was called. It was early in the morning, and we were on the main floor. When the Code II is called, it causes all elevators to stop except for the crash cart. So you guessed it. I had to run up the nine floors (eighteen flights of stairs) with my severe chest pain. By the time we got up to the ninth floor I was as white as the patient we were to see. One of my colleagues remarked, "Blais, we are going to have to code you in a minute, the way you look." To end the story, I went back and discussed the case of the ill young boy with his pediatrician. The doctor laughingly said he was sent home suddenly after he developed a rash on his hands, and he had diagnosed the boy with the Coxsackie virus. I told him my woeful story of chest pain, and he just laughed and said, "That confirms it; young adults get pleurisy from it" and he went his way. Just as though he expected that young doctors would be like old doctors who sometimes experimented on themselves to find cures for their patients.

Oh, Devil's Grip, may I never be in your grasp again.

The Beeper

Early on as interns we felt proud and important when we finally got to carry beepers. This novelty soon wore off. As a medical student I thought nothing of it when we were in four adjacent sleeping quarters in the bowels of the University Hospital and one of the beepers would go off, and we would all wake up.

But the beepers would go off at the most inopportune times, like when we were in the bathroom (more about that later).

When you put it down, it would go off, even if you weren't on call. Like the time I was a resident and my brother was an intern at another hospital. His beeper didn't work, but he was in the hospital, and they didn't page him, but they paged me at home at 2 a.m. and asked where I was. It took 15 minutes, but I told them that they had the wrong Dr. Blais.

Now you can see why when my wife was asked why we didn't have children, she would reply, it was because our birth control was 1 in 3 pediatric on call.

The beepers soon became the bane of our existence. Sometimes my tired, overworked fellow interns would hurl it, and the beeper would fly across the room and hit the wall, only to go off and say they were needed in emergency, without even a scratch on it. But it met its death by drowning when two of my colleagues, after a long night on medicine call, were paged about some inactive order. One of the interns promptly stuck it into a glass of water so that it could no longer beep, and it was gone to the airwaves in the sky.

But the beeper would return.

On Call

This had both good and bad memories for me. Rarely, it would be great, and so that my wife could see me (once in a while), she would bring over some popcorn, and we would watch TV together while waiting for the beeper to go off, as did so many other medical interns.

But often, busy, sleepless nights were more common, and most of the time this was for the good of our patients but not always. The nurses on the ward were usually very good, but some did not like to take responsibility or felt they had to do something. Sometimes after doing their rounds after midnight, they would shine the flashlight in the patient's eyes (accidentally, of course). One evening on a specific ward this happened so many times and the medical intern got upset after they called for so many sleeping pill orders that he said, "I would be awake too, if I had a flashlight shone in my eyes." He promptly left an order for the nurse to sing the patient a lullaby, and he hung up.

Also on one ward, a night nurse would urgently phone in slightly abnormal lab results which were either ignored during the day (rightly so) or that were not signed off later in the day because she wanted somebody to know, and then she would be relieved of the responsibility. In her gruff voice, she phoned the sleeping quarters of an overly tired medical intern on call about a potassium level of 3.4 (normal = 3.5 to 5.0), and he told her to give the patient a "banana STAT!" and hung up.

The calls never end!

As I said, the novelty of the beeper wore off. It was near the final days of our first year as interns. Sitting at the table at breakfast in the hospital cafeteria were six tired, overworked interns. One of us happened to be on medical call and was still on until he was relieved by another. He had had enough of the beeper. It kept going off, and he kept answering the calls. Finally he was so frustrated that he stuck it in a glass of ice water, never to beep again. The doctor promptly went into radiology, never to listen to a beeper again.

The Cast of Characters

Throughout our training, we learn many skills and acquire much knowledge, but what we remember the rest of our lives are the characters who were our mentors and colleagues. There was the family doctor who would always stop and have tea and biscuits in his office. He would show me that one should stop and allow oneself a break during a hectic day. He carried the philosophy into his life.

Then there was the Irish urologist who today thinks nobody remembers him. But how could you forget someone who would dye his hair green as the grass then wear green from head to toe every St. Patrick's Day? It was also rumoured that he was able to make his patients "pee" green on this day.

Then there was the gastroenterologist who spent time with us as a medical student and intern. He was very jovial and full of life. He was loved by everyone, but even he would get frustrated with patients or other people. His favourite line was "if he had one more neuron he would make a synapse" (a nice way of saying that person was a little dull).

There was the surgeon who the interns called "superman" because he changed rapidly from his street clothes into his scrubs and much like Clark Kent dived into his outfit. When he was on rounds, he flew around, and you had to fly to keep up with him. But when he was with the patient, he was set on cruise and always spent time with his patients and compassionately answered their questions and comforted them. As his student and later a colleague, I felt I had to understand how a human being could switch from one speed to the next.

Another surgeon gained a reputation for expecting his students and residents to be always dressed up. The men were to wear ties and dress appropriately. He detested slacks on women. One year he got on the interns so much that they came all dressed up with ties and jackets (with appropriate crests). The women wore dresses. I don't remember him getting on the interns the year after that.

The Emergency

Everybody remembers the days of rotating through the ER. We all have special names for the ER doctors: The Wall, the Sieve, Dr. Admit, etc. There were certain doctors that would rather be golfing and others that would have been golfing but were at Woodstock. One of the funniest cases I had was when an elderly patient presented to ER after getting paint in his eye. He thought he could clean it with turpentine, but that caused burning in the eye. So he thought he could use a remedy that worked at another site, and put preparation H on it. We told him that it was the "right treatment but the wrong end."

CHAPTER 2
THOSE KIDS, THEY SAY AND DO THE CRAZIEST THINGS

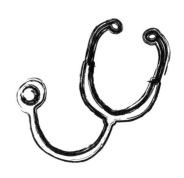

Some of the most enjoyable and funniest times occurred while looking after children. My first recollection of such an event occurred early in the first summer of family practice. One morning a mother came running into the medical clinic I was working at with a little girl with red hair, bleeding profusely from her chin. Obviously she needed stitches, and she was very scared. We got the cut sewn up, and she was sent home to have her stitches out in a few days. After I took her stitches out, her mom said that her daughter had something for me. Out of the little pocket she pulled a brownie wrapped in Sani-wrap and gave it to me. She said she had made it for me. I said thank you, and they left. As I went to examine the brownie I noticed it was rock hard! I thought to myself, she must have burned it and kept it in her pocket for one week waiting to give it to me to show her thanks!

Kids know how to embarrass you even if you are a doctor. It was my practice to examine a child's doll or teddy bear to calm them down before examining them. One night after examining a sick little girl with an ear infection, she said her Cabbage Patch doll was sick and had an earache, and she wanted me to check her. So I happily listened to the doll's chest and listened to her heart, but then I went to examine her ears and couldn't find them. The small patient offered to assist me. I sheepishly finished the examination and told her the doll was OK and they went home. As soon as I left the room I called up my five-year-old niece, Cassandra, who had one of those dolls named Loretta, and after telling her what had happened I asked her if they had tiny ears. She said, "Silly, they *have* ears. They are just really tiny. You have to look for them very carefully, and they are underneath all the wool." I thanked her for the consult.

At a later date I said to her, "Are you sure Loretta has ears?"

She said, "Of course she does. How else do you think she hears you?" I learned after that never to ask a child a "silly" question because they always had a more intelligent answer.

Next!

On another night in the office a little girl who came to see me was in her "prime." First, she walked into one of my examining rooms and asked the gentleman if he had his shirt on before she came in. After her mom ushered her back to the waiting room, she asked a gentleman to hold her ABC gum as she took the wad of the gum out of her mouth and said, "Could you hold this for me? Don't use it." The gentleman declined. Finally it was her turn to be seen. To coax her into letting me examine her I let her hold one of the teddy bears I had in my examining room. Finally after this ordeal, she ran out of the examining room and confided to the same gentleman that he could have the teddy bear next (but she wanted her gum back). The gentleman was not sure what to say and just laughed.

Passing the Test

The children always want to be helpful. One day I was examining a little girl's eyes by having her read the eye chart, but because she was too young to know her letters, I used the eye chart with symbols and objects. The little girl had trouble because she was too shy to name them. As I asked her to name each one I could not see my little patient's mouth move, but I would hear coming from behind her the correct answers, "sailboat, star", etc. Another little girl behind her thought she could not see and she should help her little friend pass her test.

Another Use for an Examining Room Drape Paper

One fall, just before Halloween, I was examining a mother and her child. I gave the mother a drape to cover up with as I left the room. The little boy hiding behind the door jumped out at me and yelled "Boo." I jumped. Here behind the door was this figure covered with a white drape looking like a ghost. The boy must have thought I wanted him to have the drape as a costume because it was the day before Halloween. Well, that drape sheet didn't go to waste.

The Terminator

In my office I have two examining rooms. I like to use diagrams and have wall posters for teaching. I was very proud of a wall poster I had called "The Body Human." It showed the anatomy of the body with the muscles stripped off the bone on one side. One day a young boy came in and was shocked when he saw the poster. He said, "Look, Mom, the Terminator." He was referring to the role that Arnold Schwarzenegger played. As I saw this boy in my office after his visit, I could hear him saying to himself, "I'll be back," with the traditional Austrian accent.

CHAPTER 3

OTHER OFFICE FOLLIES (SOME THINGS PARENTS SAY AND DO)

Early in my medical career I decided to go out on my own. However, to build a practice I needed to be available since I did not have the medical backup such as in a clinic. Therefore I needed a pager. Initially I had a pager that went off, and I had to call a number to get my message, but this became frustrating and inconvenient. I would be playing sports, and I would have to stop and run to a pay phone and find that it was not an urgent call or that somebody was paging their real estate agent and paged me by accident. Therefore I thought I'd be smart and got one that gave a verbal message out loud when the pager went off. This led to some interesting stories.

I had my office cell phone forwarded to my pager for accessibility. One day a gentleman who was very deaf called my office. I had my message on, and it was call forwarded to my pager.

So this patient received my office message, but he stayed on too long, so my pager went off. He could hear my voice on the message and said, "Hello, Dr. Blais. Are you there? Are you there? I can't hear you. Speak up." And this went on for a few minutes with him talking to my message, not realizing I wasn't on the phone. When my pager went off this whole conversation went over my pager. I knew then that he must have been phoning for an appointment to check his hearing.

Another time I was visiting the men's washroom, and my pager went off when I was at the urinal, and it was embarrassing. The man next to me said laughingly, "Mine doesn't do that."

That's when I decided to change my pager to one that had a normal message on it. I wonder why.

SOME THINGS PATIENTS SAY AND DO

Not Everything Goes Better With Coke

One day in my office a young boy was experiencing allergies, causing lots of nasal stuffiness. He felt very miserable, so I decided to give him a nasal cortisone spray to decrease his stuffiness. The boy was a little afraid and asked me what the nasal spray would feel like going up his nose. Before I could answer, his mom blurted out, "It's like getting Coke up your nose." I said, "I don't think so." She laughed, and she felt embarrassed and said, "No, no, you know what I mean, I mean Coca-Cola. When you're drinking it, and you burp, it goes up your nose." I politely said, "Yes, I understand what you mean." Her son was not any wiser, but his mom and I had a good laugh.

Memory Film

We always ask our patients if they want an appointment card after their visit to make sure they don't miss the next appointment. One day when a man was asked if he needed an appointment card he said, "Yes," and then he stated, "I have a photographic memory." So we asked why he needed an appointment card. He reported with a smile and quick wit, "But I am all out of film."

Home Away From Home

One day after a patient's wife had been very ill in a nursing home and I had been in to see her several times in the last few weeks, he boldly stated, "You know what, Doc?"

I said, "What?"

He replied, "You spend more time with my wife than I do, Doc!"

TV Controls and Determining the Newborn's Gender

Once one of my patients told me about her husband who was really excited because he had felt his wife's abdomen and the baby kicking, and it sent the TV controls flying across the room. I shrewdly kept this in the back of my mind. As I was examining her abdomen later I announced proudly, "It must be a girl." Excited, the parents said, "Yes, how did you know?" I laughed and said that it had to be because if it were a boy he would have grabbed the TV remote and not thrown it across the room. Both parents groaned and laughed. I was wrong, however. It was a boy - he must have been trying to get the controls and was clumsy and dropped them by accident.

The Natives Were Restless

One morning I was running very late and having a bad morning. The waiting room was full with people standing. In and out I went into each examining room. I started to notice that everybody was happy and talking with each other. I kept asking my receptionist in between patients if there were any complaints, and she said, "No." I was very puzzled. Later I was to find out why. As I ushered in one of my female patients to check her blood pressure, she proudly said that she was a teacher and had lots of experience in keeping people occupied. So when she saw that I was running behind, she got them all talking with each other, and they forgot about me being late for their appointments. Mrs. P. stated that "The natives were restless," but she looked after them. I thanked her.

Twisted and Warped

A patient of mine in his fifties came in to see me in a follow-up for his back problem after he had been at physiotherapy. He said the physiotherapist had told him he was twisted. He took offence and told me only his wife could say that to him. He laughed afterwards when I told him the physiotherapist meant his *back* was twisted, not him.

THE PASSING

It was a bone-chilling April morning with the snow on the ground and with the howling, cutting wind around me as spring had not arrived despite the date. This is what awaited me. I had been awakened by an ill man's daughter's call requesting that I come quickly to see her father, who lay in a hospital bed with his condition worsening. I wiped away the sleep from my eyes and quickly slipped into some day-old clothes by the bedside and rushed off. I strolled into this man's room in a dazed state from having had only a few hours of sleep. There by the bedside of this rugged but kind gentleman was his loving wife of forty-five years, whose heart had been broken by this ordeal over the past few months.

Also next to his side were his two youngest daughters, one who had called me about her father and the other with long dark brown hair who had rushed to be with him as well. The sight of their father and his shallow breathing brought tears to their eyes and faint sobbing. Despite their beauty, on this night they both appeared aged by the early morning circumstances. I felt their pain, as this man had grown to be my friend as well as my patient. But this was minute compared to their suffering, and there was no way I could tell them. The rest of the family hovered closely outside the room of sorrow. Other than the man's eldest son, the rest of the family could not bear to see him in his current state of having succumbed to the cancer.

As I watched his shallow breathing and reflected on his deteriorated health, I thought about how this man had become

DR. GUY ROBERT BLAIS

my patient. Many years earlier his internist had retired. His diabetes had been unstable, and he felt unwell. This man, who welded for a living at the time, requested that I take him on as a patient. This was my privilege, but I was not aware of what lay ahead. We got along well, as he always joked and kidded my office staff and I. This gentleman never complained and was always grateful for what one did for him, but he was sure to tell you, with his Scottish toughness, if somebody or something was not the way it should be. I respected this in him. His life had not been easy, but he never grumbled about it. Many a structure that we took for granted in our city by the river had his craftsmanship mark stamped on it. As a welder he had a strong work ethic that a job was not finished until it was meticulously perfect. This man loved his family deeply and gave to them, sometimes when he didn't have any more to give.

Through our many visits over the years, I grew to learn of the humanity of this man. Also I discovered his passion for sports, which matched or exceeded mine, and how we both lived for hockey and had been goalies in this same sport. Many a lively discussion took place between us on this topic, but now this vibrant man lay quietly in a hospital bed.

My vocation as a doctor was important to me, and if I could, but I can't, I would have wished to pass away the sorrow and enjoy the happiness of medicine. This thought was brought home to me while my mind worked as I stood by his bedside trying to comfort his daughters. Everything had been fine until just before Christmas two years ago when he was diagnosed with cancer. The ill effects of the "weed" - and probably hastened by inhaling noxious metal fumes from this trade. His doctor had told him after this operation that he was "cured." We both watched and checked, hoping this would be true, but something was not right. He was sent for tests to be done in early February of this long winter, which was made longer by these circumstances. The call came to my office late on a Friday afternoon that the biopsy was positive and the ravages of cancer had returned to his body.

Again, I reflected now at his bedside, how when I told him the awful news, he replied that he always knew there was a chance it would come back. This man, my patient, knew it was hard on me as his doctor, and tried to make me feel better when I gave him the bad news. This was just the way he was - always worried about others and how they felt.

The inevitable came to pass as his health deteriorated, and he had to be admitted to hospital. Referral was made to the Cancer Institute for their expertise in the way of treatment. With the little strength this once robust man had, he opted for radiotherapy against this "enemy." He fought hard, but his body started to fade. Then the time came when he needed more specialized palliative care. My patient was hesitant to go, but he agreed to be transferred as long as I promised to oversee him while under their care. So this was done.

It was not easy as his health faded. This early morning was extremely difficult. The night had been a difficult one for him, and now he lay asleep to the world. He was trying to grasp his last few breaths. His breathing became shallower and shallower, and we all mourned his change in health. We all anxiously awaited the priest to give him his last rites and prepare him for the afterlife. I knew that he was going to a better place, but this didn't make it any easier for his family or for me. As this man, held dear by us all, took his last few breaths, it appeared that he was just waiting for the priest to finish the blessing. As the Father concluded the final phrase, "The Passing" took place. All the family members gathered in the room around his bed, and the sound of heavy sobbing was heard, as we all missed this man greatly. He was many things to us all. Goodbyes were said to him for the last time as I tried to comfort his younger daughters and his wife.

Then I grabbed the hand of the pretty daughter with long brown hair, and I said softly that it was time to go. For this was my wife and now that my time as the doctor had ended, I became the husband who had to try to and find the strength to give her support through her grief. I had to help her through her loss and The Passing" of such a great but quiet rugged man. Then a thought came into my mind of him welding on the gates leading into Heaven and telling St. Peter a joke that he thought he hadn't heard.

The Passing was now complete.

INVINCIBILITY LOST

It just seemed like another beautiful Saturday morning as he awoke from his deep slumber, which was long overdue. Last week in the office was stressful and a day off to spend leisurely with his wife had long been awaited. As she got ready, he walked the puppy, which romped off on the leash and gladly explored the neighbourhood. He then came home and drove off with his wife to breakfast. Little did he know when he sat down to eat that this would not be any ordinary day?

As he ate, a severe dull ache came over his right chest area with a peculiar pain in his right elbow area.

"This seems like the same pain I had two weeks ago," he stated matter-of-factly and tried not to alarm his wife.

His wife stated, "They said it wasn't a heart attack."

As the pain escalated and became more uncomfortable, he blurted out, "I know it wasn't a heart attack, but not everything shows up at the time." With agony he cried, "I need to go home and rest." He then left the table abruptly for the car. She felt embarrassed because of his curt exit. "Maybe I should drive you to the hospital," she said as she set out for the car. At first he refused, but as the severe chest ache throbbed continuously, he knew he had no choice. "OK", he conceded to his worried wife.

They hit every light as it turned red and the University Emergency Department seemed to be a galaxy away. They finally arrived, and he quickly exited the car. He was perspiring now, and the pain in his chest was worse, and his right elbow ached. He must have looked like the ghost from A Christmas Carol's "Christmas Past" as he grasped his chest, and the clerk waved him on from the triage desk like a base coach sending somebody home from third. The male nurse said, "What is wrong?"

He felt like saying rudely, "Can't you tell I am pale, sweating and grasping my chest? Politely he replied he had chest pain. And again he told his story quickly about the ill-fated breakfast date with his wife.

They whisked him off to a room in a wheelchair, fearing he would collapse. Another nurse told him to get changed. He just took off his shirt and leaned over the bed in agony. He thought they told him it wasn't his heart the last time. "I must be a wimp. Hell, I have been hit around playing goal and survived worse," he exclaimed. "It's not like they say in the centre of my chest and elbow by the left arm. I must be wrong." But then he thought this wasn't going away and this wasn't like hard rubber to the unprotected chest. He moaned, hoping to get some sympathy, as he awaited the next nurse or his wife to come through the flimsy curtain, supposedly being a barrier to others hearing or seeing your misery. A nurse came in again, and he told her the story of his previous experience on May 16th after his chest pain didn't go away after walking his dog.

As he knew they were supposed to, they promptly set up the EKG (the electrocardiogram) and ran it off after attaching the sticky leads to his chest hair, apologizing profusely as they verbalized that they may have to shave the hair next time. She ran off quickly with the results of his verdict hanging in the breeze. He was now the patient. Gleefully an emergency doctor came in with a smile on his face and blurted out, "Well, this is the real meal deal. You're having a heart attack. Do you want to see your tracing?" The patient then glanced at the ST elevation on the EKG as the CO (casualty officer) yelled to send him to another room. There were nurses and doctors everywhere. His wife then walked into this masochistic scene as he blurted out, "I'm having a heart attack."

She looked at him in disbelief and then became angry and yelled, "Why did they miss it the last time"?

The doctor now the patient was not so happy with this revelation but stated, "It doesn't always show up and everything tested out OK last time." This doctor's reassurance didn't help her as she saw her husband being poked and prodded. They then went to their protocol.

"Aspirin given?"

He replied, "Yes, I had two baby Aspirin."

"Heparin started."

"Yes," somebody replied to the inquiring person who appeared to be in charge. Then the residents argued over whether to give him Fentanyl or Morphine to ease his pain. He felt like saying, "Give me drugs." When they did give him a morphine IV, it was not as he expected. He felt a little sleepy and nauseated (no euphoria).

"How bad is the pain on the scale of 1 to 10?"

He stated, "Way past 10."

"Start the nitro." The general rallied the troops and he stated, "As per protocol, his pain is not subsiding." It seemed like they knew he was game for anything, and he tried to fill his wife in on what was happening. He knew the drill. A female medical resident stepped up, asking if he wanted to be in a special study with a new clot buster. She felt sheepish as she tried to do a sales job to sell him on this wonderful drug and the study. This would then give him the privilege of getting an angiogram and angioplasty urgently just like he had won a Mercedes on Hollywood Squares. He asked her a question. "What would you do?"

She replied, "I would go for the study." He still wasn't sure if this was the research doctor or the old family doctor voicing her opinion, but he agreed. He would agree to having his chest cut open if that would relieve the pain. Then the research nurse was called in to have him read and sign the document. This was torture. He could not concentrate on the words on the paper as the pain seared through his chest and next seemed to move to the centre of his chest as he sweated profusely. I guess now it's "text book", he thought. Then another higher up resident asked if he understood what he was signing, stating that his risk of stroke, death, allergic reaction and everything else was 1 in 1,000. He still consented. Then later they sheepishly returned saying they couldn't get somebody in fast enough, so he wouldn't be in the study, and it was as if they were saying as they turned away, "You're on your own."

Then the sergeant major who was the original gleeful doctor stated, "We pissed around enough now, and let's give him TPA (the clot buster)." Then they told the patient that the risks were 1 in 1,000 for everything and of course he agreed. What choice did he have? "How's the pain?" they kept asking.

He cried out, "8 out of 10."

"Up the nitro" replied the sergeant major. And the male nurse and trainee immediately did so as his head began to throb with a headache from hell. The male nurse and trainee were pleasant and professional. But the male nurse was excited to see how the action/fun would end. The clot buster did not work. He tried to stay stoic as his wife was worried she was going to lose her breakfast date on what started off as a sleepy Saturday. He tried to explain what had happened and he knew what was next. The sergeant general, the size of Napoleon, yelled out, "How long since the TPA was started?"

"Over 90 minutes," the nurses blurted back in military cadence.

"TPA has failed. He needs a rescue procedure. I will call Cardiology and see who is on call for angiograms," he responded, as though they were lines from a bad war movie. Off flew the general with his army nearby. This left the two male nurses and his wife. His wife had to go to plug the bottomless pit metre and said she would be back. Quicker than he expected he was wheeled off to the catheterization lab as his words trailed off to let his wife know where he was going, not knowing if this important task would be completed as he visualized his wife coming back to an empty stall and expecting the worst.

As he got to the catheterization lab after winding up and down and through the labyrinth of the hospital, he was greeted by a sterile room looking like a cross between a hospital x-ray room and dissection room. He was then asked to get off the stretcher onto a strip of vinyl strapping, which was supposed to be some sort of table. The nurse stated joyfully, "I'll have to shave your groin now and maybe your chest," as she stared at the full chest of dark hair.

He replied, "I guess I'll have to get one of those Austin Power chest pieces now." She laughed, but she was not used to the other side making jokes, considering his current state. But she got the last laugh when he asked to urinate. She gave him a hard cold urinal and said to go. That is performance anxiety, he thought. He finally was able to go.

In strolled Dr. T.M., self-assured, talking about how he would like to get this done with, and he had to get back to finish his yard work, mowing his lawn, for which he could be excused for sure, as it had been raining for the past month. Then he started with questions.

"So do you have any risk factors? Do you smoke?"

"No, I don't smoke. The only risk factor I have is that I am male and overweight, but no family history of heart attacks," he replied, for he lost track of the number of times he told this same story.

Dr. T.M. replied, "I am going to freeze the groin area and put the catheter in. We'll do your angiogram, and we will find out what's wrong."

"Oh," he protested as it happened the freezing hadn't taken as he slid the catheter up his femoral artery on its way to his heart.

Knowing that the patient would ask, he gave him a Danny Sullivan play by play. "Looks like your left anterior descending artery is 'scraggly' inside," indicating this was the site of his clot and source of his heart attack. "Your right coronary artery looks like a big trunk, and it's healthy. Well, team, we are going to do an angioplasty."

Efficiently, they got everything ready, and again, he slid the catheter into a balloon up the right femoral artery around to his LAD (left anterior descending coronary artery) and somebody yelled "the pressures" as the balloon was inflating as it had been positioned correctly. To him, however, it made him think of an old movie with shipmates yelling, "the pressures" as they descended.

Dr. T.M. replied, "It looks good now. Has the chest pain lessened?" so as to reassure the patient that he would be OK.

The patient replied, "It's about 4 out of 10."

Dr. T.M., with disappointment in his voice said, "It's open now - it should be better." It was as if he expected instant relief. "Let's check this other one and balloon it." He called his order. Again, he went through the submarine submersion scenario. The patient felt actually increased pain as the balloon dilated. The patient thought, I must have given the wrong answer because it now feels like I'm being tortured. And then he gave out a yelp as his chest hurt.

DR. GUY ROBERT BLAIS

Dr. T.M. said, "We are almost finished, but I have to do a left coronary angiogram. I am going to inject a dye."

Then on cue, as if the nurse were reading her lines from some play, "You're going to feel a warm feeling spread from your chest to your extremities, and you will feel like you wet yourself, but you won't." Just as she finished her words a warm uncanny feeling opened like someone pouring warm water inside you, spreading to the groin with the same sensation she verbalized above. Then she added, "You may get some shakes afterwards, but they will go away in a few minutes." He thought she can't be lying, as he started to shake uncontrollably, and it seemed it would never stop. And it didn't for hours.

Dr. T.M. came over to him and showed him where the "enemy" was in his left coronary artery and how the after effects of his military actions of "blasting" the narrowed entry and bridging it with a splint had worked well. As if to reassure the patient again, he stated, "It may take a while for the collaterals to take over, but the pain should decrease. Everything else looks good. Having this problem must have been just a fluke."

The patient thought, oh, lucky me! The doctor thanked everybody and left.

The patient now lay there awaiting the next move. As he did go, the cardiac catheterization nurse offered to sell him the "loin cloth" as a souvenir. When he declined, the nurse asked him why, as if it were a big disappointment. Then they wheeled him off again through the labyrinth they called the University Hospital to the ICU. Finally they brought him into his "hotel room" 5C2-4. Then they transported him over to his narrow bed of rock with his set of lines and hookups that made him feel like an electrical spider. There he lay overnight with his friends Nitro, Heparin and Normal Saline. He now did not know which was worse, his back or his chest pain. Somehow he made it through the night.

Next morning, as if waking from a bad dream, he was greeted by the nurses. "Mr. Blaze, how are you?" They were not sure what response they would be getting.

"It's 'doctor," he replied sleepily, having to correct the mistake that had been made already a hundred times since coming in that fateful Saturday.

"Oh, I'm sorry. What kind of doctor are you?"

He replied, "A family physician."

She then said, "It must be hard to be in this position on the opposite end."

He thought, if only she knew, but just replied, "Yes." After asking if she could do anything for him, she went on her way.

He still lay there, not able to digest all that had happened in the past twenty-four hours. That's when the residents and students came in as an entourage with a quiet middle-aged doctor with a chart in one hand and, more importantly, his coffee in the other and his stethoscope somewhere in between. Even before getting a chance to say "Hi", he shot out to the patient, "That was a close one," as if someone had just missed scoring in overtime on the patient by hitting the post, and as the puck trickled across the goal line the buzzer went, but the puck never crossed the line completely. It was this thought that he, the patient, who was the doctor, who was I, realized that "we" were lucky to have another day to live, and I was grateful.

Throughout our lifetime we feel so invincible, especially when we are young and vibrant and think that nothing can happen to us. But something comes along and now invincibility had been lost.

CONCLUDING REMARKS

Throughout our journey through life we are touched by people, and we touch people. This shapes us as individuals and as human beings. As a physician I have been given the privilege and honour to see and do things that others can only dream of doing. I have witnessed the joy and miracle of birth and seen the sorrow and pain of cancer and death. I have tried to comfort and make the travel for my fellow human beings a lighter one. With the writing of this book, I hope I have allowed others to experience some of my privileges and honours. As Grant MacEwan (a Good Samaritan), his goal was, "If I have left this world in a better state than when I entered it, then my life has been a success." I hope you and I can say this as well.

I hope that whomever I have touched and helped along the way will be the "richer for it.
For I am the Medicine Man and this is my Rite of Passage.
I wish you Peace and Love in your hearts and God bless you.

- Guy Robert Blais, M.D., CCFP

VOLUME II
MEMOIRS
OF A CANADIAN
HOCKEY DOCTOR
(MEDICINE BY DAY,
HOCKEY BY NIGHT)

BY DR. GUY ROBERT BLAIS, MD, CCFP, FCFP

INTRODUCTION

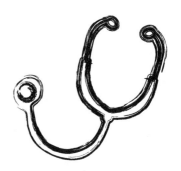

I do not know if I always wanted to be a doctor. At one time, I wanted to be a priest and a hockey player/coach like Father Bauer of Canadian International Hockey fame. Doctors and Priests do have some common functions. They both listen to people and diagnose their problems whether spiritual or other. As well they give advice to aid in regaining spiritual or medical health. Both professions are a "Calling" rather than a job. They both keep what they hear in the strictest confidence.

The closest chance I had of becoming a priest or being ordained is when some patients of mine who were nuns slipped up when speaking and called me "Father." They felt embarrassed and apologized and then called me Doctor. I told them there is no need to apologize because calling me Father is an honour in my mind.

So when did I know that I wanted to be a doctor, you ask? The seed may have been planted in my mind when I was four or five years old and my mother took me downtown to see Dr. Joseph O'Brien at his family medicine office that he shared with Dr.

Sereda. Dr. O'Brien would sit my brother and I up on stools to look through a shiny new microscope, and this sparked my interest in medicine. Ironically this same family physician who delivered me ended up giving me the exciting news that I was accepted into the Family Medicine Program, which he was the head of at the time.

As well I was interested in teaching since I had many excellent teachers over the years. Since doctor means teacher in Latin, I was given the chance to both teach and be a doctor, which were both important to me. I became a Family Physician and was given the honour and opportunity to teach medical students and family medicine residents. In this way I was able to show them the art of caring for and building a doctor-patient relationship as my practice developed. Therefore this was the best of both worlds. This is a choice I have never regretted and asked if I would do it again, I would say an overwhelming yes! It is such a special calling, where you are allowed to share in both the joy and sorrow of mankind. There is the joy of seeing your first baby born as a medical student, and there is the sadness and sorrow that you are allowed to share with your long-time patient as they battle with cancer. It is such a privilege to be able to share in your patients' life journeys, from birth to death, that as a human being you would not be able to experience otherwise. Enough about why I became a Family Physician. Why have I chosen to write these memoirs with such a specific title?

By writing *Memoirs of a Canadian Hockey Doctor* I hope to share some of the above experiences with you as well, some that are serious but many are more humorous. As well I would like to share some of my favourite writings that revolve around many of our favourite topics, which include hockey, humour and travel. You will see why I call this *Memoirs of a Canadian Hockey Doctor* (or Medicine by Day, Hockey by Night).

These are the writings of Dr. G. R. Blais (myself) with some collaboration and writings with my wife Elaine Warren-Blais from the second part of my medical career in the New Millennium. It consists of past published articles in *Stitches, The College of the Family Physicians of Canada Journal, Doctors Review* and submissions to the *Edmonton Journal* as well as some unpublished writings.

These are my experiences related to Family Medicine both in and out of the "Family Medicine Office". It reflects a Family Physicians "Real Life" shaped by their love of practising medicine and their special interests outside the family medicine office. I also share some of my insights in Family Medicine and the cycle of the speciality and its family physicians and where I would like to see it heading in the 21st century.

This book is full of my memories and experiences that I have been allowed to share with my patients and colleagues as I express them through my writings. I have had the pleasure and the privilege of practising Family Medicine in two centuries, allowing me to care for, in a few cases, four generations of families in my family practice.

I am a teacher and a doctor but maybe not a priest, but this is my vocation in life. So now let me share with you my adventures as the "Canadian Hockey Doctor".

Dr.Guy R.Blais ready to make a save.

Chapter 1
MEDICINE BY DAY, HOCKEY BY NIGHT

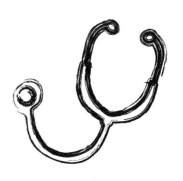

Like all Canadians, male and female, doctors and non-doctors, hockey is in our blood. It must be in our genes. Many of us dream of playing in the NHL. Some of us end up becoming doctors and play hockey at night.

I remember at age five watching Hockey Night in Canada on Saturday night with my dad cheering for the Montreal Canadiens or the "Habs" as they are more affectionately called. I lived or died with their wins or losses, as most kids did with their favourite teams. Now my team is the Edmonton Oilers.

I grew up in a community called Lynwood, where I played hockey. I was privileged to have been coached by many special men: Mr. Kelliher, Mr. Scotty Whyte, Mr. Tom Jackson and Mr. Gene Buchkowsky. They taught me more about life than just about playing hockey.

I also dreamed of playing goal in the NHL. The closest I made it was a try out for the University of Alberta Golden Bears Hockey Team when I was at university. I played for the CAC Juvenile AA Teams (TRUCO and Edmonton Motors teams) in Edmonton for three years. I played with one player who made it to the NHL (Dr. Randy Gregg) and against others that made it as well (Pete Peters and Kevin Primeau). There were a few other teammates like me that practised "Medicine by Day, Hockey by Night" including Dr. Bill Campbell and Dr. Rick Pidde. This love of hockey and medicine resulted in me writing stories about my favourite topics. Here they are!

My First Hockey Team-Lynwood Community.

Other pictures of my other Lynwood Hockey Teams.

Dr.Blais with his Hockey trophies (younger brother Greg in one picture).

CANADIAN ATHLETIC CLUB
NORTH WEST COMMERCIAL SALES — BANTAM A.A.
SEASON — 1971 - 72

TOP ROW, LEFT TO RIGHT — Marcel St. Pierre, Bob Onyschuk, Brent Crosson, Ken Kirch, Dave Galarneau, Jerry Dunn (Trainer).
CENTRE ROW, LEFT TO RIGHT — Ben Kalis (Hockey Director), Tom Lyons, Brady Mayson (Capt.), Bruce Youngman, Sean O'Byrne,
Pierre Desrochers, John Stainton (Manager).
BOTTOM ROW, LEFT TO RIGHT — Ruediger Schmidt, Randy Hill, Rolf Schmidt, Guy Blais, Dale Duperron, Ron Schamuhn.
*MISSING — Jim Jameson (Coach).

Bantam AA North West Sales CAC Team 1971-1972.

CANADIAN ATHLETIC CLUB
EDMONTON MOTORS — JUVENILE A.A.
1974-75

Front Row (left to right) Harold Bakke, Robert Hobbins, Randy Gregg (Captain) Guy Blais.
Middle Row (left to right) Harry Allen Sponsor, Vern Spallin Trainer, Tom Lyons, Brant Slaght, Don Krasowski, Jim Conlin, Brian Kortzman Coach, Norm
Vaughan C.A.C. Juvenile Director.
Top Row (left to right) Gene Buchkowsky Manager, Jim Rea, George Ford, Jim Sherstabeloof, Brian Buchkowsky, Byron Towns, Gary Barnes, Paul Cote
C.A.C. president. Missing - Terry Lee, Dean Caouette.

Juvenile AA Edmonton Motors CAC Team 1974-1975.

Juvenile AA Truco Products CAC Team- Bottom right Dr.Bill
Campbell (Teammate and later Medical school Classmate).

CANADIAN ATHLETIC CLUB

Annual Hockey Banquet
and Awards Night

1974 — 75

1935 — 1975

40 YEARS OF WORKING WITH THE YOUTH OF EDMONTON

WEDNESDAY, APRIL 23. 1975   7:00 p.m.

REGENCY MOTOR HOTEL

GOALKEEPER AWARDS
BANTAM — CLINT MALARCHUK
MIDGET — KEN BALES & ALLAN NIELSEN
JUVENILE — HAROLD BAKKE & GUY BLAIS

LEADING SCORER AWARDS
BANTAM DIVISION	MIDGET DIVISION
DON FOWLIS	MIKE SCHNEIDER

JUVENILE DIVISION
BRIAN BUCHKOWSKY

MOST VALUABLE PLAYER AWARDS
BANTAM DIVISION	MIDGET DIVISION
GAVIN THURSTON	RUSSEL FOSTER

JUVENILE DIVISION
BRIAN BUCHKOWSKY

MOST GENTLEMANLY C.A.C. PLAYER — JIM RAE

MOST VALUABLE C.A.C. PLAYER — GAVIN THURSTON

HOCKEY EXECUTIVES OF THE YEAR
BANTAM DIVISION
TRAINER OF THE YEAR — JIM RICHARDS
MANAGER OF THE YEAR — CHARLIE DOWNING
COACH OF THE YEAR — LARRY FURBER

MIDGET - JUVENILE DIVISIONS
TRAINER OF THE YEAR — MARVIN BENSON
MANAGER OF THE YEAR — GEORGE McKENZIE
COACH OF THE YEAR — DON BENSON

MOST OUTSTANDING CANADIAN'S MEMBER AWARD

CAC Hockey Banquet Leaflet 1975.

SAVING LIVES DURING THE DAY, MAKING SAVES AT NIGHT ...

I am a family doctor during the day dealing with the pressures of helping point my patients in the right direction in their search for wellness.

So this is how I relieve my inner strife: I play goal for a hockey team called the Grey Nuns (a bunch of doctors who had aspirations of becoming NHLers in their pre-medical lives). Sorry, guys. It is not going to happen. You may ask me how this is going to help. You must know my team (where back checking is not in their vocabulary).

To play goalie you have to "shut out" all your internal and external turmoil. You have to focus on the game and concentrate on the play or misplay of your team or opponents. It allows you to forget about the bad day you had at the office or the patient you were worrying about all week.

Because when your skates hit the ice and you hear the metal of your blades make contact, as you breathe in the cool air of the rink, you are transcended to another place or another time. All of a sudden you are taken back to when you were young and times were simpler and you dreamed of playing in the NHL. Your worries disappear as you start your game and glide through the crease and talk to your goalposts as Patrick Roy did.

Next you find yourself in that dream. It's Game 7 in the Stanley Cup Finals (with the series tied 3-3). Your team is up 1-0. The seconds are ticking away. All of a sudden you see a young Mike Bossy coming down on you on a breakaway. He winds up in front of you, and his slap shot is labelled for the top left-hand corner. Oh no! But out of nowhere, with the reflexes of Grant Fuhr, your glove hand goes up and you make a "miraculous" save as time runs out in the game. The crowd goes wild, and your teammates mob you. What a feeling! You have won them the Stanley Cup and lived every Canadian boy's dream.

All of a sudden when you breathe again you look up with the puck in your glove and realize you are at Sunday night hockey. You won as the buzzer goes off. Still the exhilarating feeling does not go away. Now you are ready to take on anything and get through your next week with all the trials and tribulations of our medical system. You await the next game next week to face those Bobbys, Gordies, Mikes and Marios of the hockey world as you are the goalie doctor.

In the late 1980s Dr. Brian Ritchie got "traded" from the Royal Alexandra Hospital Family Medicine Department to the Grey Nuns Family Medicine Department. At this time he started looking for players for the Grey Nuns hockey team, and he heard I played goal, and so I became one of the original members. At that time some doctors in Red Deer were setting up a Doctors' Hockey Tournament/Continual Medical Education Event to be attended by teams of Doctors from Edmonton, Calgary and Red Deer. This became a "famous" annual event starting the first Friday in February running for over twenty years until 2011, thanks to the hard work of the doctors in Red Deer (Dr. Gordon Neil, Dr. Peter Mah, Dr. Doug Simmonds and many more).

This led to me writing about my experiences during the Red Deer hockey tournaments in "Memoirs of a Canadian Hockey

Doctor" published in the April 2004 edition of *Stitches* as "Doctors on Ice." As well in 2007, I wrote a mock research scientific paper for the *CMAJ* Holiday Review entitled "Study in the inheritance pattern of the Canadian Goalie." Following this there is a tale of how looking after a patient led to my only appearance on "Hockey Night in Canada" and how this special individual continued to promote the Oilers even when he was sick. These are all included in this chapter on the topic of Hockey and the doctor. I hope you enjoy.

Making saves at night.

MEMOIRS OF A CANADIAN HOCKEY DOCTOR
Or (MEDICINE BY DAY, HOCKEY BY NIGHT)

Are you wondering where your doctors are when it is winter or early spring? They are probably away playing hockey (I use that in the loosest sense) in a Doctors Hockey Tournament in Red Deer, Kelowna or in Elsewhere, Canada. The quickest consult you will get will be in the dressing room as they prepare for the majesty on ice. Teams scheme how they will take home the "hardware" or the coveted "golden cup" trophy.

I just got back from our Doctors Hockey Tournament (15th Anniversary of the Red Deer Medical Tax Write-Off - Oh! I mean Sports Conference) as one guest speaker called it. I'm sorry, they didn't do hockey cards, but I have included our team picture for your viewing pleasure. Most of us are 30 or 30+ NHL "wannabees" hoping to make it through the tournament without an injury, and if we take home a trophy that is a bonus. Due to the hard work of the doctors and their families in Red Deer along with Tom Bast and Vi Fesik, it has grown from eight teams in the beginning to twenty teams split into two tiers now.

This is the highlight of our hockey season and, sad to say, our life every year. There have been many colourful team names over the years such as that of our team: The Grey Nuns, the NADS (short for Go-NADS), Scar Makers, Club Med, Mighty Docs, Rusty Blades, Vancouver Ringette Team, etc.

Now a little about the teams. We are the Grey Nuns Team known as the "Spirit of the Tournament." Translated:

1. We don't have a hope in hell of winning the tournament.
2. The average age of our team is probably twice that of the newer teams in the tournament (i.e. we got our MD before they were born.)
3. We bring the "spirit" to the tournament because the team that plays us knows there is a very good chance they'll get two points or at least the player will get a goal on me after the standard 60+ shots per game (but we fooled them this year and actually won a trophy in the tournament with two wins. Note that I waited until we won, so I could write this.)
4. We are the farm team for other later to be named teams.

Then there is probably no more colourful team than the NADS (Northern Alberta Doctors' Team). The rally cry chanted by their fans is "Go NADS, Go NADS" ... nothing is sweeter sounding; right? Well, except for this year when they decided to treat all their opponents pre-game and at the banquet to a rousing rendition of "Ode to the US-EH Hockey Team and Their STDs."

Then there is the Vancouver Ringette Team, who have the Legendary Boileau Brothers, some of your most loyal readers, and the other famous journal known for its articles. In the past there was the original Calgary team, which was rumoured to have try-outs for their team, and it had taken them many years before they entered three separate teams. I am surprised they had that much talent, just a little shot (you can tell I'm from Edmonton. Sorry, Chad.)

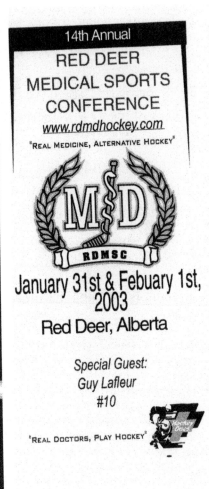

Special guests Johnny Bower and Henri Richard.

Special guest Guy Lafleur.

Also there are the Scar Masters who live up to their name in many more ways than you care to know. They are a team of plastic surgeons, other surgical specialists, star residents, past star residents and did I say star residents. For more details about this see (4) under "Spirit of the Tournament." In the past, we would joke that on interviewing potential residents for their specialty programs, the most important question was, "Do you play hockey and what level did you play at?" Again, this was only a rumour. We had the last laugh two years ago when we ended up in a higher final than they did.

Then there are the Mighty Docs of Red Deer, who have received a "nice" letter on an official NHL letterhead from The Anaheim Mighty Ducks to cease using the Mighty Docs name and logo. Gordon Neill, one of the team members joked to them that most of their players were so old that would it be OK to wait for their "passing," as they could place the sweater in the coffin and put the matter to rest. They didn't find that too humorous. I guess they could change their name back to the Central Med Army. Maybe not on second thought or they would have the Kremlin and the Russian Mafia after them.

Now, a little comment about our conference. It consists of:

1. Two games per team on Friday and two games per team on Saturday trying to resemble hockey.
2. Friday night medical symposium for core credits or see the previous name of the conference.
3. Saturday banquet and guest speaker.

First there is the draw to see who will be able to avoid the dreaded 7:30 a.m. start in some faraway arena. Despite our captain, Dr. Brian Ritchie, stating he was a good friend of Doug Simmonds, who helps make up the draw, we wound up getting two 7:30 a.m. starts in arenas that were not close to our warm hotel beds. I think Doug only pretends to be his friend, so he can give us such awful draw times. Next there were the games starting on Friday. I know you think I don't want to talk about them because we lost both games. You're probably right.

The Saturday morning pre-game started with the NADS at centre ice singing "The Ode to the US-EH Hockey Team and Their STDs." Despite this, it was a close game. I took one from #39 on the NADS for the team, no not there, but in my left chest area where my pre-1920 chest protector wasn't. My bruise continued to grow. After a later game, one of my teammates sarcastically asked me to lift my arm, so he could read what was on the puck. He started to read, "Official Red Deer Medical Sports Conference puck." We won our game against the NADS, but I had to stop whining about my injury for two reasons:

1. My wife, Elaine (our #1 fan), took a header while "fun" curling, causing her to have an Eric Lindros-like concussion, but she still showed up to cheer us on to victory.

2. One of our banquet guests was Johnny Bower, who had to "face" Bobby Hull's slap shot without a mask, and I believe he was actually hit by one according to legend. My puck-sized bruise seemed minuscule in comparison.

Johnny Bower, Dr.Guy R.Blais, Elaine
Warren-Blais and Henri Richard. `

Our final game was one of the finals against the Team US-EH (but they called themselves Southern Leafs because they didn't like the previous name). As usual the game was quite intense initially, as all Canada vs US hockey games are. Even though most of the players were ex-patriots, the goalie was from Red Deer and a drug representative from Edmonton. This intensity level rose such that one of their players called our star player, Dr. Todd, a "Sandbagger" as he easily went around him at half speed. His line mate, Dr. Peter, in defence called the defenseman a "Pylon" He took offence to that and the referees intervened and told our team and theirs that we weren't allowed to call each other names, including pylon or any other such names. So much for a compliment - they mustn't have heard of the "Pylons" team that beat us earlier 5 - 2 on Friday and went on to the "A" final. Oh, well!

Even funnier was the fact the same referees instructed Team US-EH not to swear around our team because we were a male religious order (The Grey Nuns). Their goalies set them straight and told the referees we were far from holy and only were doctors associated with the Grey Nuns Hospital.

During the game, one of their players, an ex-AJHL player, was shooting hard shots from outside the blue line from all directions hitting me in the pads then the chest and finally in the mask. What was up with this? Then I remember speaking to their pharmaceutical representative/player pre-tournament. He indicated he was playing for Team US-EH. Then he asked me where my weak spot was. Jokingly, I said "all over." He must have taken me seriously. We went on to win the game and the final and so much for the "Spirit of the Tournament" myth.

Now I have to make the readership believe that we actually went to the Sport Medicine Conference to learn and not just to play hockey and have a few beers. Dr. Peter Mah goes to great expense to ensure that we don't leave Red Deer without some new medical pearl or two. Here are some examples. The radiologist of our team learned what amenorrhea was in the female athlete from Dr. Kevin Wiebe, after he sheepishly asked what it was before the talk. Dr. Komjathy gave us an ED update: is longer and is faster really better - referring to new ED meds on the block - on "Where are your minds." These are really the actual titles, and there are more.

Dr. Rob Korbyl, an Orthopaedist, gave us a lecture on new treatments for osteoarthritis in the middle-aged athlete, where he taught us how "plugs" could be used other than for those follicle challenged players on Red Deer. And who could forget the rousing lecture hosted by Pamela Anderson given by our infectious disease colleague, Dr. Mark Joffe. It was entitled "Hepatitis C Risk after she bit you during a hockey fight." He explained that in current medical literature there was no documented evidence of any player getting Hepatitis C in that manner. Then he went on to tell us how soccer players got Hepatitis C from sharing needles used for performance enhancing medications. Next were the top ten lists of things that people didn't know about Hepatitis C. For example, the risk of getting Hepatitis C from a needle stick accident was rare (Maximum 1.8%). Then he went on to tell us that Naomi Judd was an ICU nurse before her musical fame and got Hepatitis C during that time. Hmmm! That's reassuring. But how's that for "Pearls"?

Now all you doctors who actually attended the conference but did not partake in "higher learning," (i.e. had prior commitments at the Keg) if you actually audited for claiming the course as a deduction, you may use the preceding "true" nuggets. But please don't use them again next year; some people other than you actually read the course brochure.

Who can forget the banquets over the years? From the "Incoming Scud Years" (i.e. buns away) causing them to stop having them at the tables. But it didn't stop a couple of my teammates, Bow and Sherlock, going out to Safeway nearby and having their own supply the next year to add to the festivities.

Then there were comics such as Bowser and Blue who wowed us with their music during "The Ode to Colo-Rectal Surgeon" and their comedy with the impersonation of Prime Minister Chretien during the skit of "A Proof is a Proof is a Proof."

As well, we have had the pleasure of having such legends such as Gordie Howe, Eddie Shack, Yvan Cornoyer, Guy LaFleur, Henri Richard and Johnny Bower grace the tournament. One time Eddie Shack sporting a black Stetson was playing against our team and circled around my crease. He told me I reminded him of Johnny Bower. I gleamed after the compliment even though I wasn't a Maple Leafs fan. That was fine until I asked him why he would say that and he snickered back that he hadn't seen a pair of Cooper goal pads like mine since Johnny Bower played. Promptly after that I got my wife to get me a new pair of goalie pads.

Then there was Gordie Howe, who during his honorary coaching job told his team as it was getting slaughtered that he had never seen hockey players this bad, including women's hockey.

As well as the legends we had Walter Gretzky give us a banquet talk. He started off his speech by saying he had to go on the road to talk because he never got a chance to do so at home. At the least I thought he was joking. Also to everybody's delight he signed pucks and memorabilia W. Gretzky and told us nobody would know it wasn't his famous son's autograph if we didn't tell.

Last year Guy LaFleur was razzed about his promotion of Viagra, but he laughed it off.

Guy Lafleur with myself and Elaine.

Yvan Cournoyer with myself and Elaine.

This year Johnny Bower and Henri Richard were our gracious guests. Johnny Bower was so animated and full of anecdotes, but Henri Richard was quiet until a lady in the audience asked where Johnny Bower's weak spot was. The Pocket Rocket then stole the show that evening by responding without missing a beat, "Between the legs." It was the first time all night that Johnny Bower was speechless.

So this is where my memoirs end. As a kid I started off wanting to be like Fr. Bauer and be a priest coaching Team Canada. The closest I got to that was being called Father by the nuns I look after and playing with a pair of goalie pads with Bauer emblazoned on them.

If the above piece doesn't make sense or if it appears I was rambling, blame it on a doctor and goalie taking one too many slap shots to the head. So now our patients will know where their doctors are but try finding them. They are learning about new medical advances mixed in with a little hockey. It is fitting to leave you with the thought of Stompin' Tom Connors singing "The Good Old Hockey Game."

Hope to see you at one of the doctors' hockey conferences next year.

Happy scoring (but please not on me).

The Doctor Goalie of "The Spirit of the Tournament"

PS: I won the award for the Most Sportsmanlike Player of the tournament. Have you ever heard of them giving that to a goalie? After reading this, they might think about taking it back. But I'm not worried for this will go to print after my plaque is safely applied to the trophy. Or will it be? Oh, well, there is always next year.

Hockey Cards for Top Row-Dr. Brian Ritchie, Dr.Mike Bow and Dr.Rob Kruhlak. Bottom Row Hockey Card of Dr.G.R.Blais, Dr.Peter Mah and Dr.Tony Williams.

Edmonton Grey Nuns Hockey Team-February 1992.

Edmonton Grey Nuns Hockey Team-February 1993.

Edmonton Grey Nuns Hockey Team-February 1994.

Edmonton Grey Nuns Hockey Team-February 1996.

Edmonton Grey Nuns Hockey Team-February 1998.

Edmonton Grey Nuns Hockey Team-February 1999.

Edmonton Grey Nuns Hockey Team-February 2000.

Edmonton Grey Nuns Hockey Team-February 2002.

Edmonton Grey Nuns Hockey Team-February 2006.

Edmonton Grey Nuns Hockey Team-February 2008.

Edmonton Grey Nuns Hockey Team-February 2009.

Edmonton Grey Nuns Hockey Team - February 2010.

The Enucleators: Myself, Dr. Dave Cote and the future Ophthalmologists with their manager in the back at the Saddledome at Molson Game Day Experience 1999.

STUDY ON THE INHERITANCE PATTERN OF THE CANADIAN GOALIE

Guy Robert Blais, MD, CCFP, FCFP

Abstract

Background: It is often said that goalies are a "different breed." Therefore I set out to study if there was a specific inheritance pattern for a goalie, specifically a Goalie gene (GG).

Method: Unorthodox study of a small cohort of "related" families in Alberta to study the above hypothesis of the existence of a Goalie gene (GG) in the Canadian goalie.

Results: Seven Goalies were studied in the cohort. One individual had been both a lacrosse and hockey Goalie. One individual had only been a lacrosse Goalie. All Goalies were male; there were no female Goalies in the study. Statistics and predictive interval and specificity and sensitivity are for you to figure out. They are too complicated for this author to care.

Interpretation: No specific inheritance pattern was discovered. De novo mutations and traits were considered. The Goalie gene (GG still remains the "Holy Grail" of the genetics community. As everybody knows, Goalies are a "different breed".

For many years geneticists and NHL Hockey scouts have tried to discover the inheritance pattern of the Canadian goalie. It remains elusive as the Holy Grail of the genetics community was what is commonly referred to as GG (the Goalie gene). It is a commonly held belief that Goalies are a different breed.

Recently it has been well documented there is a "factory" turn-out of French Canadian Goalies who have specific properties of the musculoskeletal system, specifically in the knees, allowing them to play a butterfly style. Have they discovered the GG (Goalie gene) i.e. performing genetic engineering or is the gene just more pronounced in that population? The author therefore set out to research the above.

GENOGRAM

Genogram for the above study.

(G) = Hockey Goalie
(LG) = Lacrosse Goalie
(Note: Ages not included)
* Author

METHODS

Model Structure

Author developed a model of a genome of related families in Alberta identifying the goalie, both female and male, and in different sports (G = hockey goalie, LG = lacrosse goalie and SG = soccer goalie) but genetically looking at the hockey goalie inheritance pattern(s).

Model parameters

Demographics and screening parameters were all Canadian (no European or Russian analysis). Just ask Don Cherry. Genogram used to document above. The data from the genogram was assessed with: **1.** Basic genetic concepts; **2.** Mendelian pattern of inheritance; **3.** Exceptions to the rules **a.** penetrance; **b.** expressivity; **c.** x interaction; **d.** de novo mutations; **e.** mosaicism; **f.** inbreeding; **g.** imprinting; **h.** law of heterozygosity; **i.** mitochondrial inheritance; **j.** phenocopy; **k.** chromosomal disorder; **l.** complex traits.

Results

The genogram of the Canadian families studied was reviewed. Of those studied, eighteen were males and fifteen were females in the cohort. There were no female goalies and seven male goalies. One, the author was both a hockey and a lacrosse goalie. Five others were hockey goalies and another was a lacrosse goalie. Note the high percentage of male goalies 7/18 (38.88%). See genogram Diagram 1. No specific inheritance pattern can be found except in certain families. The Goalie gene seemed to skip a generation, however, not following any specific Mendelian pattern.

Interpretation

As noted above, no specific inheritance patterns were discovered. However, de novo mutations were considered. This is when a genetic diversity arises "out of nowhere". This was a strong possibility since, as you all know, goalies have "complex traits" and are affected by their environment (i.e. flaky). "The traits also run in families, but do not follow any Mendelian pattern of inheritance because they are not due to single gene defects. Instead, they are brought about by a complex interaction of multiple genetic factors and the environment." [3] However, the special medical occurrences of French Canadian goalies is still a mystery to be discovered. As well as the occurrence of two generations of goalies back to back such as in Mr. Denis Brodeur and Martin Brodeur. There needs to be further studies.

Therefore, in summary, the author's conclusion is that Canadian goalies are a "different breed" and that until further research uncovers the GG (Goalie gene) it will remain the Holy Grail of medical genetics. But you all know that, anyway.

This article has not been peer reviewed as Martin Brodeur was not available due to training camp obligations.

Competing Interests

Author Dr. Guy R. Blais may be biased by the fact he is one of the members of the cohort (see Diagram 1)* and is a goalie. However, he wished that he had consulted for Bauer Hockey Equipment, so he could get some new goalie equipment, especially those new goalie skates that are so badly needed.

REFERENCES

1. Moffet, G. Moffet's Crease and Style Analysis, Goalies' World Magazine, Nov-Dec 2004, Issue 50
2. Brodeur, M. Interview Martin Brodeur (Reflection ...), Goalies' World Magazine, Nov-Dec 2004, Issue 50
3. Nasser, N. Sasseville D, et al. Basics of Genetics for the Practising Dermatologist. Dermatology Rounds, 2007: Volume 6, Issue 2.

Correspondence to: Dr. Guy R. Blais or Grey Nuns Goalie Fan Club, c/o Elaine Warren-Blais, 6138 90 Avenue, Edmonton, AB, Canada, T6B 0P2

Mr. Bill Hunter preparing to leave for the Oilers
Hockey game from Unit 42 Grey Nuns Hospital.

FOR THE LOVE OF HOCKEY AND THE EDMONTON OILERS (BUT ALWAYS A SALESMAN)

This story has been written with the permission of Mrs. Vivian Hunter (wife of Mr. Bill Hunter), so I could relate this tale of "Wild Bill" Hunter and his love of hockey and the Edmonton Oilers and how we crossed paths. I had the privilege to know "Wild Bill" in his latter years, and I knew about the stories of his fiery spirit like his red hair at the time and his ability to "wheel and deal." He was ultimately instrumental in bringing the Oilers to Edmonton, first, to the WHA then the NHL. This would result, as most Edmontonians agree, in Edmonton becoming an even bigger sports city and an important Canadian one as well. It was his will and his personality that helped accomplish this dream, fulfilling his favourite quote. This was always repeated twice as follows, "It is not your aptitude, but your attitude which determines your altitude in life." I also had heard he had mellowed over the years just as his hair was no longer red but now silver.

Mr. Hunter, unfortunately, became ill in his latter years, but this did not lessen his will to better his favourite team the Edmonton Oilers. During this time I had the privilege of being his Family Physician. His illness led to his admission to the Edmonton Grey Nuns Hospital. As Mr. Hunter stabilized medically, he requested if he could attend an Edmonton Oilers game against the Maple Leafs. This would involve much planning with the hospital and the Oilers. The Edmonton Oilers graciously with the blessing of Mr. Patrick Laforge and the magic of their public relations lady arranged for him to attend in one of their sky boxes. However, it was stipulated by the hospital that he must have a physician and a nurse in attendance. I gladly volunteered along with Sue Marshall RN (a huge hockey/Oilers fan). We did this without compensation. It was arranged for him to be transferred by ambulance with both of us in attendance to the lower entrance of the "Coliseum". There we were met by the Oilers staff and taken to the sky box.

As we wheeled "Wild Bill" to the elevator, Pat Quinn (coach of the Maple Leafs) came over to say hi. Mr. Hunter had coached him when he played for the Edmonton Oil Kings (first edition). Mr. Hunter wished him well and Pat hoped he would feel better soon. Finally we got on that special elevator to the sky box and got Mr. Hunter settled overlooking his arena.

This was a special Saturday night with the Leafs (an original six team) playing the Oilers with many of the teams faithful in attendance in their jerseys. In addition it was telecast on "Hockey Night in Canada." As the game started the broadcasters somehow knew Mr. Hunter was in attendance. They announced him and wished him well as a bright spotlight shone on him in the sky box as if he was a rock star. There was no time for me to get out of the way. This was the first and last time that I would be seen on "Hockey Night in Canada." This was a boyhood dream of mine, but I did not expect for it to happen to me as a doctor. After this monumental event for me, we tried to settle in for the game.

This was short-lived as two businessmen from a Northern Alberta town entered the sky suite, with the permission of the Oilers, to view it as they had interest in buying it. To their delight they recognized Mr. Hunter and started talking to him. A light went off in "Wild" Bill's head, and he knew why they were there. He then started his sales pitch stating how this was the best sky box/suite with the best sight lines in the arena to watch the game and how they would not be disappointed if they purchased it from the Oilers. And yes, they would not regret it as it would bring much enjoyment to them and whoever attended the game with them. Also it would be good for business. I'm not sure if he meant theirs or the Oilers. Since Mr. Hunter had just written a book of his memoirs, which he happened to have with him conveniently, he was quick to sell them signed copies, with a short note to each of them. The two businessmen left with smiles as they contemplated the words of the "ultimate salesman."

Fifteen minutes later during the next period two businessmen from Lloydminster, I believe, entered the sky suite. Again, they were pleasantly surprised to see Mr. Hunter. Quickly his focus shifted from the hockey game, and he again, saw the opportunity to sell the sky box to them on behalf of his beloved Oilers. I watched again as he gushed about the "virtues" of his Oilers sky box and why they should buy it. After he signed a couple books for them, they too went away happy. Then "Wild Bill" finally got to see the game he came to see. Everything went smoothly after as we returned him back to his hospital room, where he had an Oilers blanket draped over his bed. We did not think much more about the happenings of that night, but it would be a night I would never forget with my appearance on "Hockey Night in Canada."

A few weeks later after his strength built up, Mr. Hunter asked again if we could arrange with the Oilers for him to see another game. So again, I called the special lady who worked in the public relations department of the Edmonton Oilers. After exchanging pleasantries I let her know that Mr. Hunter had asked to attend another hockey game in the sky box he loved so much. This was the one that they so gratefully allowed us to have the other night. There was a silence on the other end, and when she came back on the phone she sheepishly said, "Dr. Blais, that sky box is no longer available." As I questioned her why, she stated it was sold the next day after the last game we attended with Mr. Hunter. She obviously could not tell me who bought it. I paused for a minute and smiled to myself thinking that it was probably two businessmen from somewhere in Alberta that had bought it. I knew despite Mr. Hunter feeling ill, he continued to promote hockey in Edmonton and particularly his Edmonton Oilers, which he loved so much that he sold the sky box right from under himself. The story ends happily with the parents of Ryan Smyth allowing us to watch the game in their sky box arranged by the special public relations lady for the Oilers.

There is a bit of tangential story related to Mr. Hunter, myself and his Oiler friends. When Mr. Hunter was in hospital, Wayne Gretzky and his dad, Walter, came up to visit him. It was quietly during the day, so I did not get to meet them. The nurses took pictures with them on nursing station 42 (which they kindly sent me). It showed how Mr. Bill Hunter was loved by so many people and especially "hockey people." What if the Oilers never came to Edmonton? Where would Gretzky have ended up? I never got to meet them then, but I had met Wayne before that and his dad after the above occurrence.

Wayne Gretzky with the nurses and the unit
clerk on Station 42 Grey Nuns Hospital.

Walter Gretzky, Wayne Gretzsky, Mr. Bill
Hunter and Visitors on Station 42.

Wayne Gretzky with Mr. Bill Hunter.

It is a small world. In the spring of 1983 in Edmonton during the hockey playoffs, I was having dinner in a small downtown restaurant in Edmonton with my wife, Elaine. There we spotted Cam Tait seated by himself, so we went over to talk to him. Cam and I knew each other from both growing up in the Lynwood community. Cam would probably say neither of us grew up. He was known as a writer for the *Edmonton Journal* and the *Sun* also for the sports section. As we were talking, Wayne Gretzky walked in with Vicky Moss, his girlfriend at that time, and spotted Cam and came to talk to him. Cam started talking to Wayne giving him a hard time as only Cam in a joking way could do. He told Wayne he was cheering for the New York Islanders. That was the year the Oilers lost to them in the Stanley Cup Finals before winning it the next year. Wayne's jaw dropped.

I cannot remember how Cam introduced Wayne to Elaine and I, but I remember him telling Wayne I was a "brain surgeon" just in case he needed one. That was only time I met him. Many years later Elaine and I met his dad, Walter, as he was the guest speaker and coach at our Red Deer Doctors Hockey Tournament in February 2000. As he signed W. Gretzky on a puck for Elaine, he told her she should say Wayne signed it and that nobody would know the difference. He was a real character in a good way.

Signed photograph from Walter Gretzky.

So it is strange how people's paths cross and do not cross and sometimes in unexpected circumstances. These stories show how hockey and practising medicine have intertwined in my life leading me to meet many special people, including Mr. Bill Hunter and the Gretzkys causing us to cross paths over the years. This is, again, why my memoirs and stories are titled *Memoirs of a Canadian Hockey Doctor (or Medicine by Day, Hockey by Night)*. Or in this case both at night.

Dr.Guy R.Blais, Mr. Bill Hunter and Dr.Jennifer Upitis.

Wild Bill in charge at Oilers' opener

It's a small world. Bill Hunter's doctor, Guy Blais, plays goal on the Grey Nuns hockey team.

"(Blais) says he used to play against me when we were kids (bantam or midget)," chuckled Hunter's son Bart, and a former Oil King net minder, who's now in the agent business.

Blais accompanied Hunter to Jari Kurri's game on Oct 6 and wasn't about to convince Wild Bill to leave before he was ready. People expected Hunter to depart after the first period to conserve his energy after a trip to the rink in an ambulance.

"Not a chance. Nobody was getting the old guy out of there (private box)," said Bart Hunter. Wild Bill stayed for the whole game.

And he was back for Thursday's Oiler Avs' game.

"You should have seen the nurses on Dad's hospital floor when (Wayne) Gretzky showed up Saturday morning to see him."

"Were they impressed or what?"

Article from the Edmonton Journal, October 7, 2001

Collage of photographs taken at Jari Kurri's game compliments of Mrs. Vivian Hunter (produced by Don Metz).

Dr.Guy R.Blais, Mr. Bill Hunter and Family and Sue Marshall R.N.

Chapter 2

TEACHING THE NEXT GENERATION AND THE EVOLUTION OF FAMILY MEDICINE

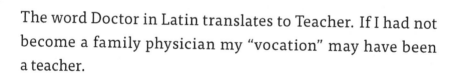

The word Doctor in Latin translates to Teacher. If I had not become a family physician my "vocation" may have been a teacher.

I have been blessed with many excellent mentors and teachers throughout my medical career, starting with my first year medical school anatomy professor, Dr. Ken McFadden, continuing into my third and fourth year with my Family Medicine preceptor, Dr. Doug Armstrong. During my Family Medicine Residency, I was mentored by many excellent family physicians such as Dr. Joe O'Brien, Dr. Mel Miller and Dr. Gordon Chaytors. As well I learned my specialty skills from training with Dr. John Harvey (orthopaedics), Doctors Robert Lefebvre,

Fred MacDonald and Herry Stefanyk Sr. (internal medicine), Dr. Harold Stockburger (surgery), Doctors Ken Miller, Patrick Pierse and Bob Moriartey (paediatrics), Dr. Rick Uretsky (obstetrics) and many others at the Edmonton General Hospital whom I apologize for forgetting to name.

They taught me about medicine and how to care for patients and importantly what it meant to be a doctor always reminding me it was a privilege to be trusted with the care of our patients' health. I hope that through my teaching and mentoring of the next generation that I have brought that same wisdom to my medical students and family medicine residents.

When asked why I teach by my patients and other inquiring individuals, I hope that I do so to teach the next generation of doctors to look after us properly when we get older and need them. They laugh at my statement, but I can see they are thinking about what I said.

I love to teach medical students and family medicine residents at the University of Alberta ever since I started in family medicine in 1983. I feel a positive obligation to teach. What do I mean by that? Maybe it goes back to a statement in the Hippocratic Oath: "...to teach them this Art, if they shall wish to learn ... that by precept, lecture and every other mode of instruction, I will impart knowledge of the Art to my sons, and those of my teachers..."

I feel I have the obligation but of a positive nature to teach medical students and family medicine residents as I give back for the teaching and mentoring that I received over my medical training.

You may say that I have already repaid my debt. You probably are right. It is a positive to continue to mentor as it allows me to both practice family medicine and teach my passions in life and some may say my "vocation" in life. As well the medical students and family medicine residents continue to remind me with their joy and zest to learn and care for my patients why I have chosen family medicine as my calling and continue to teach the next generation of doctors.

I am aware that not all my colleagues feel this "positive obligation" to teach and mentor, including some family physicians. I feel it is sad since they do not realize that they have so much to offer to our next generation of doctors and so much to gain from doing so as I have hinted at above. It may be too "classical" for some physicians, but I feel the statements in the Hippocratic Oath about teaching the new recruits continue to apply to physicians today. "To hold him who has taught this art as equal to my parents and to live in partnership with him… and to regard his offspring as equal to my brother… and to teach them this art… without fee and covenant; to give a share of precepts and oral instructions and all the other learning to my sons and the sons of him who has instructed me and to pupils who have signed the covenant and taken the oath according to the medical law, but to no one else…"

HIPPROCATES

In this chapter, I hope to show how I have contributed to this by writing on important topics and as I comment on my views on teaching and how I see the family physician in the New Millennium.

Framed Copy of the Oath of Hippocrates from Kos, Greece.

DR. GUY ROBERT BLAIS

WHAT IS THE BEST WAY TO TEACH THE MEDICAL STUDENTS AND THE FAMILY MEDICINE RESIDENTS TODAY?

When I trained in medical school during the "dark ages," we learned by attending didactic lectures, memorizing important information and then applying this knowledge to the clinical situations and patients we encountered. Then we would receive feedback from our preceptors in a manner that corresponded to where they trained. Many of us remember the "Old English" way of being asked a piece of trivia about some obscure disease or anatomy site, which we would never hear of again and being berated if we did not know the answer. We all vowed we would not treat our learners like that. Therefore I do not expect us to go back to some of the archaic ways of teaching in the past. However, we can take some of the lessons we learned from the bygone era and apply them today. I will explain later.

Over time the pendulum has swung toward Problem Based Learning (known as PBL) and lectures recorded on YouTube or podcasts that usually are not attended by many medical students but available for them to view at their "leisure". The age of computers, "Google" and sources such as "up to date" have revolutionized how our medical students and residents learn and how they apply their learning to clinical situations. If they do not know something, they "Google" it or go to a resource such as Up-to-date. For example, now they do not need to memorize antibiotics and their indication and doses because they can just look it up. All they need to know is where to find the information. Is this turning the physicians of the future into "information Gatherers"? I feel this may not be the best for the future of medicine and our future doctors and their new patients.

I feel they need to be introduced to and taught the basics in the classical way, so they can use the information they gather and correctly apply it clinically. I believe the better of the two worlds is the old and the new combined. How should they learn to take a proper history? This is an art that needs to be practised in person. What about learning how to do a proper physical examination? I know there are good resources on YouTube, but they need to be practised and have a preceptor to guide them. This is not me being old-fashioned. There is still an art of medicine that can't be found on a computer.

Till recently at the University of Alberta in the Faculty of Medicine there was a program in first and second year applying these principles called Gilberts Scholars 1 and 2 (named after Dr. Alan Gilbert a renowned internship/clinician, who taught us the old-fashioned way at the bedside of the patient). A preceptor was assigned to a group of about four medical students for each year. It was his or her task to teach the group the basics on how to take a proper history and later how to perform a proper physical examination corresponding to the body system they were studying at the time. The goal is eventually to mesh all the history taking and physical examination into an organized approach. Now the medical student would feel comfortable by the end of the second year of medical school to go out on to the wards or into a clinic and complete the above task. It

DR. GUY ROBERT BLAIS

is a bit "old school" and like an apprenticeship, but it worked for my medical students and their feedback was positive. Not everything can be learned on the internet.

As well PBL is not adequate by itself. It must be incorporated with the clinical presentation. Let me explain using Congestive Heart Failure. The medical student can learn everything about CHF in the PBL, but I found the students had trouble diagnosing and recognizing the signs. What do "Crepts" sound like? Is the pedal edema significant? If they physically see a case with a preceptor, who guides them with their PBL (problem based learning) knowledge, it is now the best of the old and new. This can be applied over and over again to the many clinical settings, as they put their learning into practice. I feel I have made my point. Also the "Art of Medicine" still exists in taking a history and examining a patient, which can't be taught by PBL or YouTube in isolation. It still takes a "hands on" approach.

So I have made my case, and it is my opinion based on many years of teaching medical students and family medicine residents that there has to be a proper mix of old and new, incorporating PBL, specific didactic lectures, use of computer resources with the "old bedside teaching" skills. This way the preceptor/mentor can interact with the "learner" and patient, teaching the learner the basics of their "craft," in my case family medicine and most likely much more. This will make for a well-trained and competent medical student or resident (our next generation of doctors) to be able to care for our patients and possibly us in the future.

The following is an elegant quote that expresses what I would like our medical students and residents to become:

"At the outset, appreciate clearly the aims and objects each one of you should have in view knowledge of disease and with its cure, and knowledge of yourselves. The one, special education, will make you a practitioner of medicine; the other, an inner education, may make you a truly good man, foursquare and without a flaw. The one is extrinsic and is largely accomplished by teacher and tutor, by text and by tongue; the other is intrinsic and is the mental salvation to be wrought by each one for himself. The first may be had without the second; any one of you can become an active practitioner, without ever having had sense enough to realize that through life you have been a fool; or you may have the second without the first, and, without knowing much of the art, you may have the endowments of head and heart that make the little you do possess go very far in the community. With what I hope to infect you to infect you is the desire to have a due proportion of each."

DR.WILLIAM OSLER

Gilbert Scholars Group University of Alberta Medical School-
Annie, Bethany, Kevin, Lauren and Kevin in"Blais-ing Hot".

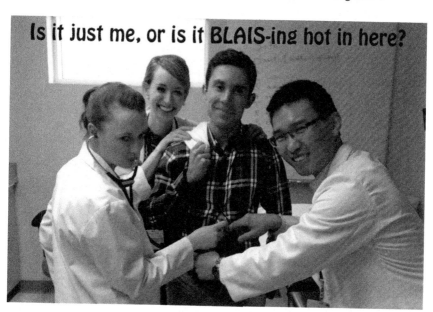

Gilbert Scholars Group University of Alberta Medical
School-Thanks for a Fantastic Year in Gilberts!!

WHAT MEDICAL SCHOOL DIDN'T PREPARE YOU FOR

(BUT YOUR FUTURE DEPENDS UPON)

Practice Management for medical students is neglected. It is not taught in medical schools across Canada, as the faculties of medicine feel there is no time for it to be squeezed in an already crowded medical curriculum. They hope that the students will be taught about practice management in their residency programs. However, this is not always the case. The exposure they receive depends upon what residency program they are in and where the program is situated. For example, at the University of Alberta, the Royal College Specialty Residents receive only a one-day course presented by Practice Solutions/ MD Management. While the Urban Family Medicine Residents at the University of Alberta have a two-day program sponsored by the same group, which I am involved in. I present day one with a representative from Practice Solutions.

Due to this deficiency in our medical training for practice in management, I felt the need to address it with, first, the checklist that appeared in the newsletter for the department of Family Medicine of the University, # 36, summer 2001. In the introduction to it I remarked, "As I teach, I learn more and more from the medical students and residents that they are ill-prepared in many aspects of starting a medical practice since it was not taught to them in medical school. Such aspects as choosing and setting up practice, getting specific insurance and minimizing unpreparedness are important. Therefore I dedicate this article to the medical class of 2001 and those who follow, so they will be better prepared to go forward and enjoy life, consistent with what I believe is a vocation of medicine."

Since that time I have presented to the Faculty at the University of Alberta/Department of Family Medicine on Practice Management. As well I presented on a number of occasions the same topic to the Medical Student Family Medicine interest group at the University of Alberta.

To address the concern nationally, I also submitted a paper on this topic to the *Canadian Family Physician*. It was published in the June 2004 journal.

I have included both of the articles I discussed above in this chapter as well.

WHAT MEDICINE SCHOOL DIDN'T PREPARE YOU FOR

(BUT YOUR FUTURE DEPENDS UPON)

"As I teach, I learn more and more from the medical students and residents that they are ill- prepared in many aspects of starting a medical practice since it was not taught to them in medical school. Such aspects as choosing and setting up practice, getting specific insurance, and minimizing unpreparedness are important. Therefore I dedicate this article to the medical class of 2001 and those who follow, so they will be better prepared to go forward and enjoy life, consistent with what I believe is a vocation of medicine."

Dr. Guy Robert Blais MD, CCFP

1. Where to Start

- Choose a good family physician, a good lawyer, a good accountant and a financial adviser.
- Don't forget your friends, and more importantly, don't forget your family.

2. Choosing a Residency

- Specialist vs family physician. Do an elective to check out your choice. Lifestyle, type of medicine, hours of work, noting that practices vary with the doctor who runs them.
  - Canada vs. USA (preferred province or state noting that where you do your residency is most likely where your immediate opportunities will be)
  - Rural vs. Urban Practice Preparation
  - Residency Placement - Same university vs. other
  - Don't forget your significant other or family in your decision process.

3. Developing a Life plan

- Career (personal goals)
- Family
- Spiritual
- Financial Goals
- Hobbies
- Health
  The order may vary from doctor to doctor but develop a life plan as early as possible.

4. Insurance

Get what you can and start early if you can.

- Life insurance more easily acquired while problem-free and young, can be increased without penalty for condition and chosen with advice on advantages of Term/Whole Life in the amount a trusted adviser suggests.
- Personal and Office Disability Insurance sufficient to cover expenses while off work with a critical illness, with specification of no job except as a doctor in your field noting the waiting time for payment.

5. Setting up Office Practice

- Rural vs. Urban
- Solo vs. Group
- Area demographics
- Office only vs. office and hospital privileges or hospital beds
- On call arrangements
- Choosing an office

6. Where to Get Help?

- Financial/Practice Oriented: CMA (Canadian Medical Association; MD Management (CMA related); Don Price & Associates; Colleagues; AMA (Alberta Medical Association); Financial Institution (practice start-up loans with bank); College of Family Physicians of Canada and their resources

- Health (Medical/Mental): Family physician (you should all have one); Physician Assistance Program (Medical Association operated)
- Medical Protection Liability: CMPA (Medical Legal Advice) or equivalent
- College of Physicians and Surgeons (or State Licensing Board) can be used as a reference
- Ethical and Spiritual: Religious or spiritual leaders; Hospital or University ethics department, pastoral care; Reference material, including *The Healer's Calling - a Spirituality for Physicians and Other Health Care Professionals* by Daniel P. Sulmasy OFM, MD, *Principles of Biomedical Ethics* by Tom L. Beauchamp & James F. Childress, *Health Ethics Guide* by Catholic Health Association of Canada.

7. Holidays and Hobbies

Holidays and time off to "recharge batteries" having the next break in mind. Hobbies and non-medical refreshers for the mind and body such as reading, sports and outside interests make for well-rounded individuals.

Copies of the entire article, including references can be obtained from Dr. Guy Blais at 780-469-5533. Originally published in Educating Tomorrow's Family Physicians, University of Alberta Newsletter of Department of Family Medicine, #36 Summer 2001

DR. GUY ROBERT BLAIS

PRACTICE MANAGEMENT WHAT MEDICAL SCHOOL DIDN'T PREPARE YOU FOR (BUT YOUR FUTURE DEPENDS UPON)

Guy Robert Blais, MD, CCFP

As I was getting ready to attend my twenty-year University of Alberta medical class reunion, I pondered what medical school had not prepared me for and what I wish I had learned. I dedicate this article to the medical classes of the New Millennium.

Where to Start

- Choose a good family physician to look after you.
- Choose a good lawyer, preferably a general lawyer whom you can talk to and who can refer you to others for more specific legal concerns.
- Choose a good accountant. Interview candidates and make sure they understand tax issues for physicians and are readily accessible (ask for references from other physician clients).
- Choose a financial adviser (sometimes serves as insurance broker as well) with appropriate training. The Canadian Medical Association has MD Management.
- Do not forget your friends.
- More importantly, do not forget your family.

Developing a Life Plan

Life plans are optional; some find them too structured. Various physicians have written about the life plan concept.[1] Important considerations are:

- career (personal goals)
- family (Will you marry? Will you have children?)
- spirituality[2]
- financial goals (for a comfortable lifestyle, for retirement, etc.)
- hobbies (outside interests keep the internal fires burning)
- health (without good health, other goals are meaningless).

Insurance

Get as much of each type as you can and start early.

Life Insurance

- When you are young and have few medical problems, it is easier to get coverage.
- Get riders to increase amounts without penalty for illness.
- Learn about term, whole life and universal coverage.
- Consult your financial adviser for amount of coverage you need. Rather than deciding on a lump sum, consider what after-tax income a surviving spouse would require for the next thirty years.

Disability Insurance

Individual or personal disability: marital status and having children will affect the amount needed. Premiums are affected by age at application and other factors. Insurance needs are also determined by earned income after business expenses but before taxes.

Table 1. How earned income affects insurance needs

Earned Income ($/MO)	Minimum Allowable Benefit ($/MO)
2000	1420
4000	2610
6000	3660

Waiting time for payment: Know when policy takes effect and when payments begin (times vary). Remember there is always another thirty-day wait for funds (i.e., waiting time thirty days, first cheque at sixty days). Disability coverage should be occupation specific, that is, you are considered disabled and will be covered unless you can go back to your previous field of medicine as a doctor (not back to another occupation).

Critical illness insurance: This new type of insurance provides lump sum payments for serious illnesses such as heart attacks or strokes.

Office overhead coverage: Amount depends on staff and overhead expenses (review with changes in office). Policies state whether you must wait for a thirty-, sixty-, or ninety-day period before coverage starts, again, with a thirty-day waiting period until first payment. Awards are usually paid out over eighteen to twenty-four months.

- The amount you choose might depend upon income available in your business.
- Insurers require you to show receipts.

Other (car, house, medical office insurance): Medical office insurance covers office interruption, liability for injuries on-site, fire insurance, floor insurance, theft and so on. If you insure your car and house as well, some insurance companies give discounts. Check with your local medical association.

Review: All insurance policies should be reviewed regularly to keep coverage up to date. Discuss with your broker when this should be done. I suggest yearly.

Setting up office practice

Consider doing electives or locum tenens in potential locations.

Rural vs. urban. Consider:

- isolation vs. support
- type of lifestyle
- available activities
- privacy
- on-call coverage

Solo vs. group. Solo practice is less common now because of costs and isolation. Consider:

- your personality type
- others' personalities and quirks
- costs
- on-call practice coverage
- contracts
- Locum trials to check for compatibility with personalities and type of practice.

Area Demographics

Office only vs office and hospital privileges

On-call arrangements. To cover your practice obligations.

Choosing an office. You can:

- build a new office to your specifications
- choose existing office space and make improvements
- lease or buy property

Other matters. If you need a bank loan to set up practice, having a business plan helps in obtaining it and shows you are prepared. The plan should outline your cash needs for:

- equipment
- staffing
- start-up funds
- projected income
- other unexpected expenses

Office Management

Staffing

- When hiring, arrange interviews so that you can give applicants your undivided attention. Make sure you know the terms of contracts with staff.
- Firing employees is unpleasant. Employees can be fired, but it is best to consult a lawyer beforehand. This is why it is important to interview properly to have a probationary period and to have contracts outlining your expectations of employees.

Salaries (in 2004)

Be prepared to conduct negotiations with prospective employees. Examples of usual salaries (MD Management and your local medical associations can give you up-to-date ranges) are:

- Office Manager $20/h
- Nurse $20/h
- Medical Receptionist $10-$15/h
- Filing Clerk $10/h.

Benefits

- Sick days: Employees are entitled to one day/month.
- Health care and dental coverage are commended but not required.
- Workers' Compensation Board enrolment is not required for medical offices but should be considered.

Holidays and maternity leave

Labour laws. Know the labour laws for your province. Consult a lawyer about what is important in hiring and firing.

Billing

Insured Services

- Provincial health care billing organizations
- Workers' Compensation Board

Uninsured services

- Third-party insurers require certain paperwork.
- Post standard fees in the office.
- Guidelines for uninsured fees are available from provincial medical associations.
- Remember to discuss your policy with patients.

Where to get help

Financial and practice oriented

- College of Family Physicians of Canada
- Canadian Medical Association
- MD Management for financial and practice management
- Provincial medical associations
- Financial institutions

Ethics and spirituality. Several publications[2-4] suggest ways to address values in practice.

Health (medical/mental)

- Family physician (you should all have one)
- Physician Assistance Program (medical association operated)

Medical protection liability. The Canadian Medical Protective Association or equivalent can offer medicolegal advice.

College of Physicians and Surgeons. Provincial Colleges of Physicians and Surgeons and state licensing boards function for patient protection but can be used as references.

Conclusion

These are some considerations for practice and financial management. I hope they will serve as a resource for my future colleagues-to-be, so their transition into the "real world of medical practice" can be smoother.

Acknowledgement

I thank Dave Greenlaw of Financial Focus in Edmonton, Alberta and my many mentors at Edmonton General Hospital/Grey Nuns Hospital, Misericordia Hospital, Royal Alexandra Family Clinic and the Faculty of Medicine and Dentistry at the University of Alberta. I offer special thanks to Dr. Gordon Chaytors and Dr. Joseph O'Brien for guiding me to this point. Finally I thank my sister, Denise Blais, and my wife, Elaine Warren-Blais, who both encouraged me to write about my experiences during my medical career.

References

1. Nedd K. What they didn't teach us in medical school (Residents' Page). *Can Fam Physician* 2001;47:801
2. Sulmasy DP. *The Healer's Calling: Spirituality for Physicians and Other Health Care Professionals.* 1st ed. Mahwah, NJ: Paulist Press; 1997.
3. Catholic Health Association of Canada, *Health Ethics Guide.* Ottawa, Ont: Catholic Health Association of Canada; 2000.
4. Beauchamp TL, Childress IF. *Principles of Biomedical Ethics.* 3rd ed. New York, NY: Oxford University Press; 1989.

LIFE CYCLE OF FAMILY MEDICINE DOCTORS

Dr. Guy Robert Blais

On November 25 to 27, 2004, I, along with other Canadian family physicians, celebrated the 50th Anniversary of the College of Family Physicians of Canada.

In the past I have reflected on the life cycle of the family as we care for our patients from birth to death. I deliver the newborn and support the grandparents as they deal with the "golden years".

As I was at the ceremony for our new Certificants, Fellows and Life Members, I thought about the life cycle of family medicine and family doctors.

On this day, Dr. W. D. (Doug) Armstrong (a past Family Physician of the Year) was receiving his life membership certificate. He had just retired from his family practice. He was my family physician and one of my mentors. I first spent time with him as a medical student, learning about family medicine in his office and at the Misericordia Hospital in Edmonton, Alberta. Doug encouraged me to proceed with my career in family medicine.

On the day of the ceremony, as I received my Fellowship along with my classmates and colleagues, I pondered how we have taken over the role of our preceptors and mentors and how we are passing on the torch of family medicine as we teach and learn with medical students and family practice residents. This was just what our predecessors and mentors had wanted. They were the grandparents, and we were the parents of the family medicine family.

On this same day, there were many new Certificants of our college. I had taught a number of them on their journey in family medicine, but for me Dr. Manickavasagam Sundaram (Mani) receiving his certification stood out. I had known him from his first days in medical school during his "shadowing" experience all the way to the time he spent in my office during his family practice block in 2003. I hope I gave him fatherly support to continue with his career in family medicine, and I hope I will continue to do so in the future.

Now it is time for our new Certificants to take over the family medicine torch as the sons and daughters of the family medicine family. And I am filled with enthusiasm for them as they start their new careers in family medicine. May they kindle in their medical students and family practice residents the same excitement and the quest for knowledge and the well-being of our patients that was passed on to us from their grandparents and mentors of family medicine not that long ago.

As we have just celebrated a special year for family medicine in Canada, reflect on your own family at home and our other family, the family medicine family. May we support, encourage, and thank them both, and may the life cycle of family medicine doctors continue to prosper like the families of patients that we care for each day.

Footnotes: Articles from *Canadian Family Physician* are provided here courtesy of the College of Family Physicians of Canada.

CHANGING FACE OF FAMILY MEDICINE

We are not celebrating the 60th anniversary of the founding of the College of Family Physicians of Canada (CFPC). There have been some important changes in family medicine and what being an FP encompasses in the 21st century. After reading the well-written articles about these changes in the January 2014 issue of *Canadian Family Physician* [1-5], I was moved to reflect on how I would like to see the FP evolve. These articles included those on Dr. Ian McWhinney and how his and others' visions have shaped family medicine, as well as what the authors thought Dr. McWhinney's wishes would be for the CFPC as we go forward.

I do not profess to have the wisdom and insight of Dr. Ian McWhinney and the authors of the recent articles, but having taught and practised family medicine in Canada for more than thirty years, I would like to give you my wishes and hopes for the CFPC and for FPs in the 21st century.

Protect the underlying theme of the comprehensive FP. I am well aware of the subspecialties in our college and the good they do in helping our patients. In addition, I know that the day of the all-inclusive FP doing hospital care, obstetrics, and paediatrics along with an office practice has faded. But we must continue to train our family medicine residents to look after the "bread and butter" medical and psychosocial conditions that we endeavour to help our patients with every day. With no disrespect to our fellow specialists, some have become so sub-specialized that they only look after knees or ears. This is not the way I would like us to venture.

Promote family medicine as a career choice. We must continue to promote our specialty of family medicine with passion through teaching of and encounters with medical students, residents and colleagues. The exposure to these groups through teaching is important to this concept and cannot be overemphasized.

Improve the balance in our lives. We must accept the fact that our younger colleagues appear to have a better balance between their personal lives and professional lives than we ever had. They are sharing family medicine practices, and both "father FPs" and "mother FPs" are taking time off to be with their newborns. We should embrace this balance and refrain from using the classic line "I remember when I was ..." We should learn from their example.

Support one another. We should all have our own FPs that we can rely on for our health needs. This support should start at the medical student level. As well we should try and help one another when our health or that of our family members fails. We should also assist our colleagues who need a break or time off because they are afraid of burnout. It might involve a little extra work or call time, but it will be appreciated and is usually reciprocated when you need the same courtesy. We should at least treat one another as well as we treat our patients - have compassion for one another always.

Advocate for patients. We must continue to advocate for our patients, especially in these times of turmoil and disjointedness in our health care system. This is one of the most important roles we play for our patients.

Participate in continuing professional development. We should continue to learn and strive to be the best FPs possible. The manner in which individual FPs decide to accomplish this task should be up to them, as I still believe each of us understands how we learn best. This will prevent stagnation and prevent the physicians' knowledge from becoming outdated, allowing them to give the most up-to-date care to their patients.

Honour traditions. We should remember to learn from our past and from traditions. Not all that is old is wrong. For example, the tradition of the house call should not be abandoned, as it serves a purpose in certain situations. This is despite the fact that many physicians might believe this is outdated and unnecessary. I disagree, as house calls might be the only way certain patients can see FPs. This promotes continuity of care. As well, the tradition of a house call by the FP supports and comforts the patient. It accomplishes something sacred to our role as a physician.

The above is my vision for what I believe is important for FPs and family medicine. The face of family medicine might be changing in the 21st century. My vision for the new face continues to include the four principles of family medicine and is consistent with the Three Cs in the Triple C Competency-based Curriculum, but I believe it goes beyond it. I believe the above statements are important to reflect upon to help guide us forward. This will allow us to continue the strong tradition of family medicine in Canada that Dr. Ian McWhinney and others have envisioned.

- Guy R. Blais, MD CCFP FCFP
Edmonton, Alberta

Competing Interests

None declared

References

1. Pimlott N. The quiet revolutionary. *Can Fam Physician* 2014;60:9 (Eng), 10 (Fr)
2. Weston WW, Whitehead C. Why continuity matters. Ian McWhinney's insights for 21st century medical education. *Can Fam Physician* 2014;60:11-3 (Eng), 24-6 (Fr)
3. Pimlott N, Upshur REG. From clinical observation to clinical discovery. The challenge for family medicine research. *Can Fam Physician* 2014;60:14-6 (Eng), 27-9 (Fr)
4. Martin D, Pollack K, Woollard RF. What would an Ian McWhinney health care system look like? Can Fam Physician 2014;60:17-9 (Eng), 30-2 (Fr)
5. Handford C, Hennen B. The gentle radical. Ten reflections on Ian McWhinney, generalism, and family medicine today. *Can Fam Physician* 2014;60:20-3 (Eng), 33-6 (Fr)
6. Article provided from Canadian Family Physician May 2014 by the permission of the College of Family Physicians of Canada.

THE TEACHING TREE

The Tree Hippocrates taught under in Kos, Greece.

The tree has been used as a symbol of growth as well as to represent the values and qualities of certain groups and societies, including the College of Family Physicians of Canada (CanMeds-Family Medicine). It also has been the symbol of education and learning. This dates back to ancient times, including the sacred plane tree in Kos, Greece. This is where according to legend Hippocrates taught his students and residents who in turn went on to teach others spreading out like branches. Their branches then went on to teach others and to grow.

Recently as the students started back to medical school, I had been reflecting on how my teaching tree would look today having taught medical students and residents for thirty years. My roots would be diagrammed with the names of the family physicians and specialists who taught me as a medical student and family medicine resident. I am grateful to my "roots," family physicians Dr. Joe O'Brien, Dr. Doug Armstrong, Dr. Mel Miller and Dr. Gordon Chaytors and the many others who planted the seed for family medicine in me and nurtured my growth with firm support in the ground. This allowed me as I entered Family Practice to continue to grow and develop my own branches of medical students and family medicine residents as I taught. I wish I could remember them all, so I could draw out my own teaching tree and the branches and their outshoots as well. You would have thought as a young Family Physician that I would have contemplated such a project since I was always interested in mathematics. I am sure there would be some formula to calculate exponentially the branches and the outshoots that were created in my teaching tree. It would probably fill a wall.

It is not too late for some of our younger family physicians to start their teaching tree, as they teach and keep track of their branches. For those who have not started teaching I encourage you to do so. I am sure you will enjoy it as the medical students and family medicine residents challenge us to be a better family physicians, resulting in a better "skilled physician who are a resource for a defined population, which are our patients. This will remind us to continue to grow and contribute to an eternal teaching tree. This is much more than a process alone. By creating this teaching tree you will see how much as family physicians we contribute to teaching and the promotion of family medicine in our communities.

I challenge all family physicians, family medicine residents and medical students to develop their own teaching tree. They then can see how it grows, as they grow into their teaching tree and flourish as a family physician and promote teaching and our speciality of family medicine. I hope my branches and outshoots are doing well and that I have given them some strong roots as they spread out throughout our family medicine community.

It may seem old but as written in the Oath of Hippocrates, "I reckon who taught me this art equally dear to me as my parents to share my substance with him ... to look upon his offspring in the same foot as my brother and teach them this art, if they shall wish to learn." This takes us back to the original teaching tree which medicine was based on. I wish you all well in this challenge.

Dr. Guy R. Blais is a Clinical Professor in the department of Family Medicine at the University of Alberta, who works and teaches in his family practice in Edmonton. Competing interests - none declared.

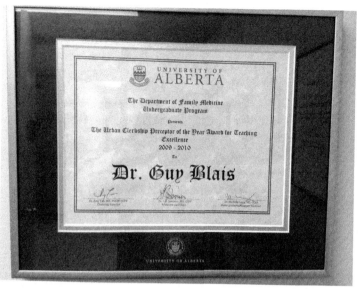

The Urban Clerkship Preceptor of the Year Award for Teaching
Excellence –University of Alberta in the Department of
Family Medicine Undergraduate Program 2009-2010.

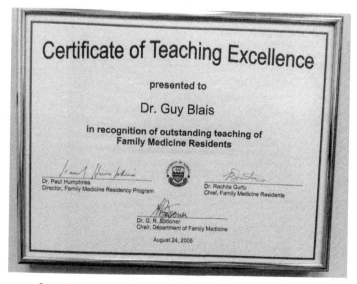

Certificate of Teaching Excellence in recognition of
outstanding teaching of Family Medicine Residents-
University of Alberta August 24,2005.

Certificate of Teaching Excellence in recognition of
outstanding teaching of Family Medicine Residents
2002-2003-University of Alberta June 30, 2003.

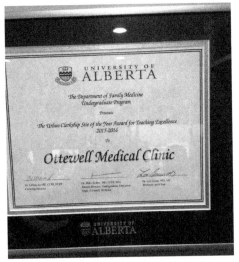

The Urban Clerkship Site of the Year Award
for Teaching Excellence 2015-2016.

UNIVERSITY OF
ALBERTA
Faculty of Medicine & Dentistry

In Recognition of Commitment to Teaching

Dr. Guy Blais

is Appointed as

Clinical Professor

Dean, Faculty of Medicine & Dentistry

Chair, Department of Family Medicine

July 2010

Clinical Professor Appointment in Department of
Family Medicine at the University of Alberta.

UNIVERSITY OF
ALBERTA

FACULTY OF MEDICINE & DENTISTRY

Office of the Dean
2J2.00 WMC
University of Alberta
Edmonton · Alberta T6G 2R7
Telephone: (780) 492-9531
Fax: (780) 492-7303
www.med.ualberta.ca

August 26, 2016

Dr. Guy Blais
6138 - 90 Avenue
Edmonton, AB T6B 0P4

Dear Dr. Blais:

You have been reappointed as a Clinical Professor in the Department of Family Medicine effective July 1, 2016 to June 30, 2021.

I wish you every success in your collaboration with the Department of Family Medicine.

Yours sincerely,

Richard N. Fedorak, MD, FRCPC, FRCP (London), FRSC
Interim Dean, Faculty of Medicine & Dentistry

cc. Dr. Lee Green, Chair, Department of Family Medicine

/wb

Reappointment as Clinical Professor in the
Department of Family Medicine at the University
of Alberta July 1.2016 to June 30, 2021.

Chapter 3
TALES FROM THE OFFICE - SOME AMAZING OR NOT

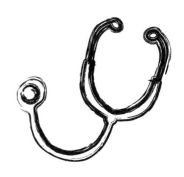

Even after thirty years in family practice, patients can still walk in with stories that amaze me. The first is a story of survival in what seemed like an impossible scenario. The others are those about patients with "amazing" ideas. I hope you enjoy these tales.

Do You Believe in Miracles?

It is late on a Friday afternoon just before the Labour Day long weekend, and my last patient of the day hobbles in on crutches. The twelve-year-old boy and his mother are here to have me check on a wound on his left leg. I start to ask how this happened, and his mother begins by saying that her son had been run over by a truck. She then interrupts herself and encourages her son to tell me what had happened.

He begins, "My friend and I were on our bikes at a crosswalk and a driver in a truck saw us but thought we were not going to cross. He didn't check again as we went to cross. My bike and I got dragged under his truck. I hung on to the side of his truck and runner board, and I was under it with my bike."

His mother then interjected that she was told people were yelling at the driver, but he didn't hear them until her son had been dragged eight metres under the truck. I could not hide my shock and blurted out, "Oh my God!"

I asked, "Do you believe in Guardian Angels?" She stated that there had been some divine intervention, and that this was a miracle. The mother then went on to say that when the fire department, EMT's and other people saw that he son was not hurt other than a scraped right knee and a small wound on his left leg, they all called him a "Miracle Boy."

I then shifted back into my doctor persona and asked if he was wearing a helmet, and she said yes. I also asked if he had any signs of a concussion, headache or dizziness, etc. He said no.

The boy then continued to relate his tale how he hung on to his bike as he was dragged and that it was a sprocket on his bike that had dug into his left lower leg. Nonchalantly he said his bike was destroyed, but he would be getting a new bike.

I finished my examination and confirmed what they had been told in ER was correct. That all he had suffered was a swollen unbroken left leg with an uninfected wound, which now had two stitches in it. I listened as the boy talked just like a twelve-year-old boy, essentially unaware that he had cheated death.

After changing his dressing, I gave him and his mom advice how his left leg should be re-checked and x-rayed if the leg swelled on the weekend. His mother agreed to do that.

As they left his mother looked at me and said, "It is certainly a miracle." I said nothing but thought certainly it was and that his Guardian Angels were working overtime on that day. I have never seen or heard of this happening to any of my patients in my practice of over thirty years. Yes, I believe in Miracles.

Selective Hearing

An older Scottish gentleman presented to my office one day to have the wax cleaned out of his ears because his wife had noticed he was not hearing that well. Everything went well until it came time to see if the procedure had worked and that he could hear again.

So I enquired, "So can you hear better now?"
In his Scottish accent he replied, "Pardon me?"
So I asked again, "Can you hear better now?"
Again, he replied, "Pardon me?"
I was a bit confused now since I know both his ear canals were crystal clear now. I asked him for a third time, "Certainly you can hear better now since the wax is all gone."
With a smile he replied in his Scottish drawl, "Certainly I can, Doctor. I was just practising for when I get home."

This is just a little Scottish humour and "selective hearing."

The Stool Sample

An elderly gentleman in my family practice told me how he got back at some elderly ladies at a nursing home. He found these ladies were preoccupied with their bowel habits. They would be asking each other about when they had their last bowel movement and how large it was and what colour, and they went on and on about them. They were obsessed with this topic, and the conversation always came back to this topic.

So one day he brought in a small black container that was used to store film back in the day. He labelled it on the side "stool sample." As the ladies were getting into their daily conversation about their bowel movements, he cut them off and said, "Would you like to see my stool sample?" Then he promptly went to open the container as he watched the ladies' faces go white. Out this gentleman pulled a miniature wooden stool with four legs. He laughed at the look on their faces and the ladies never brought up the topic of BMs (bowel movements) again.

Now whenever I have a new medical student or family practice resident in my office, he asks me if I have shown them his "stool sample." Usually I say yes and that I have it stored in a special place.

The Stool Sample.

Chapter 4
ADVENTURES/ MISADVENTURES IN MEDICAL TRAVEL

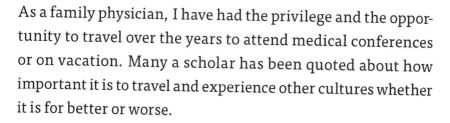

As a family physician, I have had the privilege and the opportunity to travel over the years to attend medical conferences or on vacation. Many a scholar has been quoted about how important it is to travel and experience other cultures whether it is for better or worse.

I will relate to you how I have experienced other cultures and express my views on my medical travel experiences with my wife Elaine. Some of these will be in humour and some are more of a serious nature.

Here they are. Please enjoy as you travel with me.

VIENNA WAITS FOR YOU

As we walked into our room and turned the TV on, Billy Joel's "Vienna Waits for You" floated across the airwaves. The couple in the video were enjoying the many spectacular sights and sounds in Vienna. From that time forward, the song that we heard so many times became our anthem for our stay. As our tour members did the classic Viennese dinner and visit to the opera house, we set out on our own to do the unorthodox Wien.

There are many non-traditional attractions available to you and yours in Vienna, the old Ottoman Empire capital. So let us tell you about our adventure.

The first night we went to their year round fairground, which is adorned by a large Ferris wheel. It is famous for having survived a bombing, which had taken place by mistake during the World War II. From here you get a beautiful view of Vienna at night. For the children with you or in you, there are many rides and culinary delights available at the typical fairgrounds at VolksPrater. After we rested up overnight, we went with our group to see the sites of Vienna, including St. Stephen's Cathedral and the Anker Clock, but we took a pass on visiting the Schönbrunn Palace, and we ventured off on our own for the afternoon.

Off we went to a medical museum hidden in Vienna known as the Vienna Institute of the History of Medicine (the Josephinum). This is the original site where in 1785 Emperor Joseph II founded the academy to train his field surgeons. To do so he had Isodore Canerale construct the complex called the Josephinum. As well the emperor commissioned a collection of anatomical and obstetrical wax models for their study. This was created in Florence between 1775 and1785 under the supervision of the anatomists Felice Fontana and Paola Mascagni. (This collection was transported to Vienna and made its way actually to Brenner Pass on mule back and down the Danube River from Linz to Vienna.) This is how the field surgeons learned their anatomy.

In 1920, Max Neuburger moved into the building with his own medical and historical collections. His support came from none other than the famous cardiologist Wenckebach. The Josephinum was made into the traditional site of Vienna Medicine and the Art of Healing in Austria. Erna Lesky became the director and head of the institute in 1960.

The Josephinum.

As stated in the brochure given to you during your tour, this made it "a place of pilgrimage for everybody interested in the history of medicine." These are the words of Erna's Zurich colleague E. H. Ackerknecht.

The museum consists of:

1. The Welcome Room - Vienna Medicine from Era of the Enlightenment to the "Vormarz" (up to the March uprising in 1848). This comprises the beginnings of clinical teaching, including Dr. Avenburger, who is said to be the inventor of percussion. (As well there are examples of the instruments of the army surgeons of the 18th century.)

2. "Modern" Vienna Medicine Room presenting the Vienna Medical School of the 19th and early 20th century. It has representations of each of the specialties or fields of medicine and their doctors of the time, including Bilroth and Freud. In this room there is also a display of stethoscopes that were the personal possessions of the Vienna physicians such as Wenckebach.

3. The Josephinum library, houses non-medical and medical books that date back to the 15th century from many of the renowned authors of the middle ages and the Renaissance. It also houses the more recent books on surgery and anatomy.

4. The most impressive collection of Anatomical and Obstetrical wax models. They are kept in their original "Rosewood" and glass cases. The room is kept at a specific temperature for preservation of the masters. The exquisite

detail of the dissection replicas is amazing and reminds you of Dr. Netter's drawings.

The museum is housed in an exquisite building bordered by an iron rod gate. As you enter you are greeted by beautiful roses and a lush green courtyard and you may wonder if you are actually in the right place. Talking about the right place, make sure you take the far right door that is clearly marked. We mistakenly went into a part of the building that was probably verboten. However, we got to view a collection of old stethoscopes and instruments. As well, we saw an example of the medical lecture room with approximately a hundred seats, which appeared to be still in use.

Collection of old Stethoscopes of Dr.Wenckebach.

The importance of this museum may not be immediately understandable to us North American doctors, but Vienna was once the capital of the Ottoman Empire, and therefore this was the beginnings of modern medicine in Europe (outside of the British Isles).

The official name is Museum du Institues fur Geschichte der Medizin der Universitat Wien (Josephinum). The address is 9, Wahringer Strasse 25, Wien, Austria (Vienna). Tel. 4277-63 401: Hours Mon. to Fri. 9 a.m. - 3 p.m. (except holidays) and first Saturday every month 10 a.m. - 2 p.m. I suggest taking a taxi to get there, but it can also be reached by tram.

Now, if you are exhausted or your companions are, you need to go by a short taxi ride to Landtmann's Kaffe, the favourite café house of Dr. Sigmund Freud, and have a leisurely lunch. Don't forget to try their Landtmann Eis Kaffe and for dessert Fruchtebecher.

Now that you are refreshed, you can walk to Volksgarten Vienna, approximately two or three blocks away. Ask your waiter for directions and use your Vienna map, which is available at your hotel front desk. Here you can stop and "smell the roses". This is the people's garden with a beautiful park lined by many different types of roses in neat rows with names such as Queen Elizabeth, Rumba, etc.

If you like to do more sightseeing, there still is the following:

Non-Medical

1. Hofburg Palace (Helden Platz)
2. Natural History Museum
3. Maria-Theresias Platz

(All near Volksgarten, within a 10-15 minute walk)

Medical or Semi-Medical (I suggest you go by taxi.)

1. Sigmund Freud Museum at 9, Bergane 19, Wien (Vienna). Open October to June, 9 a.m. to 5 p.m. and July to September, 9 a.m. to 6 p.m. Guided tours available by appointment (Tel 319 15 96) (www.freud-museum)
2. Sigmund Freud Park

When you have explored enough, you could travel back to your hotel by horse and carriage (located throughout Vienna, including at the entrance of Volksgarten). The horses are beautifully groomed, sometimes decorated with ear coverings. The cost for a ride is determined by the distance and length of time of the ride. It may seem extravagant, but it is the classical Viennese transportation.

Horses and Carriages lined up in Vienna.

As you travel back home, you probably will be unable to get that song out of your head, for "Vienna waits for you."

P.S.: Acknowledgements to:

- Billy Joel for his song "Vienna Waits For You"
- The people of Vienna for making our stay so memorable
- The staff at the Josephinum Museum for the information given to us through their brochures of this amazing medical museum, including the curator who so kindly supplied my wife with a copy of the museum brochure in English.
- As well for the ability to take pictures in the museum where it was not verboten.
- The use of a map of Vienna (Wein) and information from city map

If you are going to Venice next, like we were, and would like to experience a little Italy in Vienna, then you have to spend the evening at Galateria Café Perella Eis Salon, a small Viennese Italian sidewalk café, and have a Tramezzini (Italian sandwich). But more importantly save room for the huge ice cream and fruit dish called Romeo and Grisilleta. Life is so sweet, and Venice is another journey.

Edited version published in Doctors' Review February 2006 as "I prescribe a trip to … Vienna"

The Volksgarten in Vienna, Austria.

VIVA LAS VEGAS OR NOT

(Or the trip I wouldn't recommend)

As you may be aware, there is a publication that publishes the writings of trips recommended by doctors. I actually submitted an article about the trip my wife and I took to Vienna.

Well, this is the opposite. I would like to enlighten you on a trip I would recommend you do not take.

I will try to tie this in with medicine. You all know the reason for that.

It all started one recent spring day when my wife, Elaine, shocked me with a surprise early anniversary gift. She told me we were to meet for lunch. At lunch Elaine told me we were to meet with our travel agent, Jayne, as we were planning a trip to Greece later in the year. Much to my surprise, she and Jayne then broadsided me about a surprise trip to Vegas. They were afraid I would code on the spot, for the trip was to see Elton John in Las Vegas in the near future, like the next day. I guess I must have had a strange look on my face. Jayne kept saying, "Dr. Blais, are you okay? Dr. Blais, are you okay?" Afterwards, Jayne told my wife she wasn't sure whether I was angry or whether I was totally overwhelmed by their conniving. The latter was the case. The look on my face was probably just foreshadowing what was to come next.

We went to the airport the next day after rushing to pack for a long weekend. There we met a number of Alberta psychiatrists on the same flight. This included one that was my past medical student. I must have scared him off from Family Medicine because after spending time in my office, he entered a psychiatry residency. Or could it have been that he saw so many interesting psychiatric cases in my family medicine practice that it inspired him to make this career choice? Yet again, no ... oh well, they were going to Las Vegas as well, and my wife went over to find out where they were staying. Again, you don't need to ask why, but my wife has a running joke with me that I could always tag along or show up at the conference then "write off" my trip. Please don't tell any of the Revenue Canada people. It's just a joke, really. But the joke was on me. I should have taken her up on the suggestion. I would have gone with them to a suburb of Las Vegas where the conference was sponsored by some "split personality" drug (you know, it couldn't make up its mind whether it was for depression or for quitting smoking).

But being the honest doctor I am, I went off to see Elton John. When we arrived in Las Vegas, my wife discovered that somebody had gone through her bag. And nobody would take the responsibility for doing so. Unhappily, we left the airport.

So then we shuffled off to a famous Las Vegas hotel represented by a Lion's Head. There the front desk clerk checked us in. He thought he was giving us a jewel of a room when he assigned us to the "West Wing." He advised us that these were new rooms, and we would love it. People especially liked the fact they could watch a plasma TV located in the mirror in the bathroom. I thought, wow, I really wanted my face superimposed on a TV!

So we trekked off and I mean, trekked off to the room located two miles from the desk. We had trouble finding the room because somebody had ripped off the number on the door. Once we decided counting with our fingers that we were in the right room, we entered. To our amazement the room was in disarray and looked like it had been trashed by a rock star. We quickly shut the door and did our marathon back to the desk. There we were greeted by a dismayed desk clerk even after we explained our findings. So we told him the West Wing wasn't like on TV and not to our liking in this hotel. We asked him for a room only one half mile over from the desk with a Lion's Head on the door. He gave us a puzzled look after we told him we did not check on the "Voyeur" bathroom.

The next night we got to see Elton John as planned by my secret agent wife, and it was a fantastic show, and I thought our fortunes were changing. How wrong was I, as we had booked a bus tour to see the West Rim of the Grand Canyon the next day? My mid-life crisis must have been kicking in, as I thought this to be one of the Seven Wonders of the World and a place you must have on your list of places to see before you die. However, it also must have been in my horoscope that I wasn't to go to any place with the word West in it. My wife was less than enthusiastic. She said she had a bad feeling about this. Stupidly, I said it would be okay. I think I should have bought the Corvette instead to settle my mid-life crisis.

The tour of the Grand Canyon was going smoothly until after the Hoover Dam we hit some construction. The sign was posted for 25 mph and our driver, Eddie, crawled along. Then we hit smooth pavement, and he started to cruise. Out of nowhere our tour director announced that the long arm of the law was pulling us over. There we sat for 15 minutes. As the unamused bus driver climbed back onto the bus, he told his sad tale of woe. Eddie was told by the officer in a congratulatory manner that he did go 25 mph through the construction area, but he wasn't allowed to go faster when he hit the hard top, as technically he was still in a construction zone. He was clocked going at fifty mph, and he was given a ticket.

As we approached the West Rim of the Grand Canyon we had to travel on a fourteen mile dirt road. Our bus and its occupants bounced around and we inhaled dirt until we got to our destination. As we neared the West Rim it started to snow, and it was fogged in. So we were not unable to see the true scenery of this Seventh Wonder of the World. Our tour bus driver remarked this was strange as the weather was beautiful yesterday, and it had not snowed up here for two years. Wouldn't you know it! After we took pictures of the imaginary Grand Canyon we stopped for lunch at the Native Centre. The helicopters were grounded as well, and luckily we hadn't booked a helicopter tour of the Grand Canyon. Originally we were to have a barbeque out near the Grand Canyon at a special site, but the weather nixed that.

After lunch, as we settled on the bus, our tour director indicated we were going to make a rescue. There was a tour group that had come up by helicopter some time before the fog. They were stranded now because there was no way out by air. So our new fellow travellers settled in. My wife said she felt it was like the Partridge family meets the Griswolds.

We left the Grand Canyon West Rim, and we travelled along the fourteen mile dirt road. There the road was showing the effects of the spring run-off from the mountain streams. There were large holes in the road. The tires and bus they supported were taking the brunt of nature's erosion. Shortly after the driver announced we had a flat tire from all the jostling. Luckily (that is, I think that was lucky), we were able to continue at a snail's pace as he radioed ahead for a replacement bus to meet us at our morning stop.

The tour director, Bill, continued on undaunted with his "spiel" and stated we were going to stop and take a picture of the "Joshua Tree". Bill then announced it was rattlesnake season. Suddenly he gleefully pulled out a fake rattlesnake from a box, but not to everybody's delight. He explained how we should be careful and try to avoid them. We should also carry a rattlesnake kit with us, and he showed us his unopened one. I thought, great, I was going to be able to write the trip off after all as the medic for the bus tour from hell.

Bill continued by saying that if we got bitten, we should stay calm and find the sturdiest, sharpest piece of metal we were carrying, which for most people were their ignition keys. Things began to look more promising, surgery on the bus and a free trip to Sin City.

The tale went on and he then stated that it was going to hurt, but you would have to suck it up and have to jab it in … (he paused). Bill then laughed out loud and quickly said jab it into your ignition and get yourself fast to the nearest hospital. My heart sank. I knew I should have gone to the drug conference here with the psychiatrists. The tour finished without any further disasters.

The rest was history as they say. We got home and I lived to tell about the trip. I would not recommend a trip to Las Vegas and the Grand Canyon, but that is okay. I didn't lose a lot of money at the casinos because I had no time to do so for reasons explained above.

Happy Travels to someplace else and remember to bring your rattlesnake kit and good weather with you.

By Dr. G. R. Blais (with contribution from Elaine Warren-Blais)

THE "TIJUANA EXPRESS"

In the 1990s when we were attending a medical conference in San Diego, my wife Elaine and I decided to take a Gray Line bus tour to Tijuana.

The tour started in San Diego and went around the various hotels to pick up our fellow travellers for the adventure. It happened to be that one of our stops was a hotel holding a medical convention. It was here that about ten individuals got on, including some anaesthetists and their wives. We overheard there was a major national anaesthesia conference at this hotel. They did not know I was a fellow physician, and I did not care to let them know as well.

Everything went smoothly as we left San Diego and crossed the Mexican border into Tijuana. The male bus driver was an experienced driver who made sure all the passengers knew the planned itinerary. As we entered downtown Tijuana the bus stopped in front of a Mexican restaurant, where we were going to have a planned dinner. The bus driver clearly told us all that we had one hour for dinner and half an hour for shopping. We were also to meet at 7:30 p.m. sharp at the same spot. He wanted to leave Tijuana at that time to miss the heavy traffic of people travelling back across the border to San Diego. He stated he would leave then, and he hoped we would all be on time since in all his years doing this tour he had never had to leave anyone behind. Foreshadowing, as my English teacher once said.

So we all had a wonderful Mexican dinner in Tijuana, but as we finished dinner, two of the male anaesthetists told their fellow conventioneers that they were off to find their "holy grail," a leather covered armadillo shaped footrest. Their fellow colleagues cautioned them that they had to be back by 7:30 p.m. As these two gentlemen left, they laughed and said not to worry as they ran off down some alley on their quest.

As 7:30 p.m. came the driver drove his bus up to the spot in front of the Mexican restaurant, where he asked us to meet him. He promptly did his head count and found there were two people missing. The worried but experienced driver asked if anybody knew where these two men were, and if they saw them. A few of the colleagues related to the bus driver about the quest of these lost souls.

The driver decided to wait a few minutes, but after a while when they did not show up at the meeting spot, he left. Then he proceeded to drive up and down downtown Tijuana asking all the passengers to let him know if we spotted them. After a futile hour of no sightings, the visibly shaken driver indicated he had to leave. The driver could not believe after all his years of driving that tonight he would have to leave somebody behind. He explained that for the other passengers' safety and to respect their time he had to leave.

Now we were late making it to the Mexican/U.S. border from Tijuana. He advised us we would have to make a detour. "A detour?" I enquired. Yes, he explained that we had to take a detour since we left so late and the line-up at the border with all the vehicles returning to the USA would take hours to get through, and he did not want us to be any later than we already were. The driver indicated he was going to use a seldom used short cut. He then proceeded to go down what appeared to be an unpaved switch-back road, but before he did this, he said he would be turning off the lights in the bus and asked us to stay quiet to avoid detection by the border security. It appears we were taking a road to reach the USA San Diego Border in a clandestine manner. After 15 minutes on this serpentine road, we came to a metal fence closed by a padlock and "manned" by a Mexican boy probably no more than ten years old. The bus driver quietly paid the boy, who let the bus pass through the gate to the other side, and he promptly locked the gate.

The driver then took us on the bus close to the Mexican/USA border crossing where he thought it was safe enough to let us off to cross by foot through security as was the custom. He then said he would be waiting for us with the bus on the other side without stating how he was to get through the huge line of traffic in front of him.

We all crossed the border into San Diego, USA without any problem, and he was there smiling waiting in front of the bus as we exited the security building. We still do not know how he got his tour bus across the border to meet us. Perhaps there was another mystery gate, or did he know somebody, who let him in line out of queue.

Needless to say, Elaine and I will never forget the "Tijuana Express."

Dr.G.R.Blais holding Oath of Hippocrates in front of the Temple of the Roman Age 2nd-3rd Century AD in Kos, Greece.

THE "HIPPOCRATES EXPERIENCE"

In September of 2005, my wife and I had the pleasure of travelling to attend a European Family Medicine Conference in Kos, Greece. As we landed at the Hippocrates Airport the warmth of the sun greeted us on this beautiful Greek Island, which is actually closer to mainland Turkey than Greece. As all physicians should know, Kos was the home of Hippocrates and the birthplace of modern medicine according to "legend". This was the place Hippocrates taught his students under a Plane tree for many years.

We were quick to learn that this may have been the birthplace of medicine, but it certainly had not kept up since some modernization needed to take place here. Let me try and explain why.

The Mayor of Kos was kind enough to arrange for a special celebration for the conference attendees, which took place at the ancient site of the Greek gods of healing. What occurred was a recreation of an ancient ceremony of healing that took place at this site. This was complete with maidens dropping rose petals along a pathway with Greek music playing, followed by a healer/physician reading aloud in Greek from an ancient text.

This was all very pleasant except it was an extremely hot day, and the area was "paved" with uneven stones. This did not help my wife who was having trouble with her ankles and feet. She had humoured me by attending this ceremony and went along anyway. Later she walked with me to the area where Hippocrates taught under the Plane tree (now, unfortunately, supported by green iron girders). Here too the same ancient walkway existed in uneven stones.

Needless to say by the time she arrived at our hotel her feet and ankles were swollen and painful. We then tried to find out where we could get medical help. This is when we found out how modern the birthplace of medicine was. The concierge at the hotel explained to us that not all the emergencies in each hospital were open and that they rotated with being open. The one that was open today was extremely far away, so he advised us to do as Greeks did. I asked what that was. "Go to the closest pharmacy, of course," he replied. Who would have thought of this in the land of Hippocrates and the birthplace of physicians!

08/07/2005

Recreation of Ceremony Greek Gods of Healing
at Ancient Site of Healing Kos, Greece.

Dr.Guy R.Blais with Oath of Hippocrates
next to the Hippocrates Tree.

First, I asked if they had any crutches at the hotel, which was a negative. I took the address to the closest open pharmacy that night. As well I was given the name of the pharmacy and what lit sign indicated they were open, and I was at the correct place. From the hotel I took a taxi to this place of healing. I then proceeded to explain to the pharmacist that my wife needed a pair of crutches if they had them. I thought everything was going well when she said she understood what she needed. To my shock the pharmacist came back after dragging out some heavy metal "polio crutches" still in the "wrapping" straight out of the movie "What About Mary." I said no, I need a regular pair of crutches. She said she understood and brought out a pair of heavy wooden crutches that were relics of some cross possibly. I then questioned her if she ever heard of aluminum crutches that were light and useable, and she said she had not. I just sighed as I placed a call to my wife about the only "modern" crutches that they had at the pharmacy. She decided to take the wooden "station of the cross" crutches (no disrespect since I'm Catholic, but they were heavy). All I can say is so much for modern medicine and appliances for your health.

The next day we were having lunch at the five-star restaurant at the hotel. My wife noticed that someone had sneezed on the salad at the salad bar. She told the Maitre'D. He thanked her for her observation, and he promptly removed only the top layer of the lettuce from the salad bar and did not replace all of it. I guess Hippocrates did not teach them about the spread of illness. Oh, I guess that came later from Pasteur and Lister and company!

Finally the next night we attended a special dinner for this medical conference. There was a family physician from Canada attending as well with his wife who had asthma. So when he saw so many physicians and attendees smoking, he went up to speak to the organizer who was a Greek family physician. He kindly asked if he could make an announcement that due to the fact people like his wife had respiratory problems that were aggravated by smoking; people should refrain from smoking at the dinner. The Greek physician stared at the Canadian family physician and was taken aback by his request and said he would not make the announcement. My colleague just walked away in disbelief. There were so many Greek family physicians still smoking at the dinner and the conference despite knowing the ramifications to themselves and their patients.

So much for the Greeks learning and applying evidence-based medicine and preventing illness. This was "the Hippocrates Experience."

Dr.Guy R.Blais and Elaine M.Warren-Blais at Zia, Kos, Greece.

DR. GUY ROBERT BLAIS

Sunset on the island of Kos with Turkey in the background.

ALL IN A DAY'S WORK FOR THE AUSTRIAN FAMILY DOCTOR

At a recent European Family Medicine Conference held in Vienna, Austria, we had the chance to visit the office of an Austrian Family Physician. The country Austria is rich like the province of Alberta in Canada where I come from. That is when our oil is priced high. The Austrian medical system is based on the Bismark system. A quick summary is all Austrians have heath care coverage even those who are retired, unable to work, children or the disabled. The funds for healthcare in Austria come from "deductions" to the salaries of those who work. Entry of the patient into the Austrian Health system is unique. This family physician explained that Austrians seeking medical care for a particular medical condition such as hypertension could access it in three different ways:

1. via family physician
2. through a "community" specialist (no referral needed)
3. lastly by "hospital" specialist (no referral needed)

The patient theoretically could see all three about the same medical condition. However most Austrians do not despite the Austrian riches, as this in my opinion would lead to excessive health expenditure and collapse of their health care system.

As we went to visit this family physician's office, we saw people lined up around the block in an ordinary line in front of the entrance to an unassuming nondescript building that housed his medical office. They have no appointment system other than the patients registering with the attendant/medical office assistant as they come in and then coming back when it is their "appointment time." The Austrian family physicians usually work solo with only one attendant and no nurse. This usually female attendant helps register the patients and shows them in.

This Austrian family physician worked out of one examining room large enough to include his desk for consultation and one examination bed. He said this was typical for the Austrian family physician. Their typical hours were three shifts of three hours during the day, with breaks in between. Here they would also do their house calls, but they did not have hospital patients. Other doctors looked after the hospital patients.

An Austrian Family Physician had to be registered with the Austrian government and obtain a billing number to receive payment. But when starting their practice, the younger family physicians sometimes had to wait to receive a billing number; therefore they billed patients privately until they received the billing number.

Austrian family physicians still have their own patients, but the way the system worked for payment was unique. The family physician was paid a certain fee to care for the patient with a certain medical condition such as hypertension for a three-month period no matter if you saw them one time or ten times. However, for a specialist they were paid a monthly fee to care for a particular medical condition. So even in Austria there are differences in payment for a family physician and a specialist. So in theory the patient could see a new family physician or specialist as dictated by the above system. But in reality, just like in Canada, most patients are quite loyal to their family physicians.

The Austrian family physicians are paid in Euros, but they have to see many patients a day in order to earn a good living and pay for the running of their offices. This family physician saw minimally fifty patients per day.

This opened my eyes and made me happy to practice family medicine in Alberta in Canada with a fairer payment system for caring for our patients. "All in a day's work for the Austrian family physician" would be way too much for me.

This brings me to the end of my writing about my travels usually related to my medical conferences. Yes, travel, especially for these conferences, certainly opens your eyes. It makes you glad to come home and write about them and be happy to know you have been educated in more ways than one. I hope those who read these "tales will feel the same way.

CHAPTER 5
LOST TRADITIONS IN MEDICINE

With everything changing so fast in the 21st Century in medicine, new technology is always felt to be best for our patients and their care. This is not always the case. There are certain traditions in medicine that in my opinion should be retained. In this chapter I write about two of them, the house call and the anatomy lab, that I hope will continue to be kept. But are they lost traditions?

Maybe I am like most people who think that most doctors do not make house calls like I do. I hope I am wrong. I hope that the new family physician who is graduating will not forget about this special tool that they can put in their doctor's bag.

I also could be wrong about the anatomy lab playing a less important role as a learning tool in medical school. It is my understanding that medical students spend less time studying anatomy in the lab. Also they are not exposed to the anatomy lab until later in the first year or second year of medical school. I write how this experience affected me and my fellow classmates as well as how it has left a lifelong impression on us. Certain traditions even in medicine are important, and I hope you agree after reading this chapter.

THE HOUSE CALL (HER FIRST)

One busy Friday afternoon in my family medicine office, I was seeing patients with a young medical student during her Family Medicine Rotation. As I started to state my bias for choosing family medicine as a career I was interrupted by my receptionist stating that there was a worried daughter of one of my patients on the phone wanting to speak to me. I quickly picked up the phone and heard a female voice enquire, "When can you come out to see Mom, so we can get her set up for hospice." I paused as I thought about when I would be able to see her mother. Her mother was now no longer able to stay at home as her cancer had spread to other parts of her body making it impossible for her to do so now. But before the neural synapses could connect to respond to her she blurted out, "You need to see Dad too." I first responded that it would be better to see him in my office, but she replied, "He is too short of breath to come in." I stated "I'll do a house call at the end of the day and see your mom and dad then." She said thank you and that she would be there too. The phone call ended, and I heard the medical student say with surprise, "You make house calls!"

I responded, "I know it is an urban legend, but I do."

Then I enquired, "Have you ever gone on a house call?"

She replied with excitement, "No, this would be my first."

After we finished seeing the remainder of our afternoon patients, I briefed her on the two patients we were going to see. I indicated to her that they were an elderly couple of European descent, who were my patients for many years and that they lived nearby in a bungalow. The lady had cancer and, unfortunately, had developed complications related to the cancer spreading to her neck and subsequently her lungs. Also despite her fight with the cancer she never complained and continued to deny having any pain (stoic from her heritage?). But now she had made the decision she was unable to carry on at home and needed to be assessed for hospice care.

Just before we left my office I called their home. An elderly man, my other patient there, answered the phone, and you could hear as he spoke that he was very short of breath and was having trouble getting his words out. I knew from how he sounded on the phone that he would need to be seen too. This gentleman had a history of heart disease, but I had just recently seen him in my office, and he was in a stable medical condition. I told him we would be there shortly.

As it started to get dark out, the medical student and I ventured out on a cold January winter night to her first house call.

We navigated our way through the neighbourhood to the bungalow where our two patients awaited us for the house call. We were greeted at the door by the husband. He took us inside this comfortable warm house, where his wife was resting in an "Easy Boy Chair" in what appeared to be a spotlessly kept living room despite her circumstances. My medical student and I politely removed our boots at the door and placed our winter coats on an adjacent couch.

Quickly my medical student stated, "I hope it was OK I came with Dr. Blais."

Their son was there, and he pleasantly replied, "The more the merrier."

Slowly our "doorman" sat himself down in another Easy Boy chair to the left of his wife.

I attended to him first and asked him how he was, and he said not very well. He then said with difficulty, "I'm short of breath and having trouble talking." I asked him how long that had been going on. I was not sure if he heard me since he was extremely hard of hearing, and so the questioning was slow but done meticulously. We extracted that he had been getting more short of breath over the past two weeks. In addition his feet had started to swell, but he was still able to lie flat in bed at night. He also did reply that he did not have any chest pain in the past two weeks.

Now it was time to examine him. My medical student asked this elderly gentleman permission to pull up his shirt, so we could listen to his heart and lungs. He jumped as she placed her hands and stethoscope on him. She apologized with, "Sorry for my cold hands." I did not say anything but knowing him he was just joking around with her. This was just the way he was even when he was sick in my office and I had a medical student or family medicine resident examine him prior to doing so myself.

As well upon my entrance to the examination room he joked about how I always had someone else doing my work for me.

After this short interruption she carefully applied her stethoscope to his chest and listened intensely. I then took my turn to listen to his heart and lungs. After I completed my examination I asked my medical student, "What do you think."

She replied, "His chest is clear to me. I can't hear any crepts."

I followed with, "Yes, surprisingly his chest is clear, and there is no heart murmur or extra heart sounds."

But despite our findings our elderly patient was obviously short of breath and had some trouble talking. From the background came a voice, "Look at his feet and how swollen they are." It was his daughter who had now arrived on the scene. She continued, "It's been like this for a few days. What do think is wrong?"

I replied, "I think he is in heart failure." I then proceeded to explain to our patient in "English" that his heart was not working right and fluid was backing up into his legs and down into his feet. He nodded but I am not sure he understood the translation completely (lost in translation).

Then I apologetically told out our first patient that I would recommend that he go to the ER for treatment to get rid of the fluid that had built up in his body.

He bargained with me. "Can I wait until tomorrow morning?"

I sadly stated, "No, you should go tonight, so things don't get worse." He reluctantly agreed. The medical student kindly looked up an App on her phone to help him decide which hospital ER would have the shortest waiting time to see a physician. The discussion continued on whether he was strong enough to go by car or by ambulance. He and his family decided to go by car so they could choose their "Favorite ER".

But before this could be arranged we proceeded to examine our "star" patient who the primary house call was arranged for. There she sat surprisingly comfortably in her Easy Boy chair. We proceeded to ask her the normal questions we would ask our palliative care patients, including whether she was having any pain and where it was located. Stoically as I expected she replied she was in no pain. Then a quick but thorough exam was done. Then I focused on the main reason we were there to see her. I asked "Mrs. D, do you want to go to a hospice."

She replied, "Yes, Dr. Blais. I can't manage at home, and I can't look after my husband now." The last part she said quietly since she felt badly. However, it was unlikely that her husband would have heard her since both of them were extremely deaf. I knew it broke her heart to say this, and I could see it in her eyes. She was extremely disappointed that she could no longer carry on in her home, where she had lived for so many years and shared so many memories with her husband and family. I let Mrs. D and her daughter know that I would fill out all the necessary paperwork and send it in, so she could now go to the hospice.

After this I asked if my patients or their family members had any other questions. Mr. D asked when he should see me again. I reassured him I would see him sometime after his hospital visit depending on what transpired there. He was happy with that response.

The medical student and I gathered up our "Winter Garments" and boots, and as we left the house call recipients, they and their family members thanked us for making the house call.

As we left the house and walked over to our cars the medical student stated, "That sure was a sudden change in him." I replied that it was and something may have caused the sudden change. Next she said, "Thank you for allowing me to come on the house call."

I smiled and said, "You're welcome and have a nice weekend. I will see you on Monday." She wished me the same.

As I drove away from the house I wondered what she had thought about her first house call. Was it what she expected? Did it make her think about how important it was to the patients and their care? Did it show her the importance of keeping this medical tradition alive? There were so many more questions I could ask her about her experience. The one I would like the answer to was whether this event made her think more about becoming a family physician and that this would be the first of the many house calls she will make in her medical career. I certainly hope so. Only time will tell.

I smiled as I realized I would have to wait until Monday morning to hear what her answers would be to some of my questions. She would have the weekend to ponder about the experience of the house call maybe with her friends or fellow medical students. Maybe we will have one more convert to doing house calls and continuing this medical tradition, so it did not become an "Urban Legend".

THE ANATOMY LAB (THE CADAVER)

As we entered the anatomy lab the pungent smell of formaldehyde permeated the air. The aroma of it burned our eyes, throat and lungs. We were not ready for this despite the kind anatomy professor, Dr. M trying to prepare us for it before in the classroom. We approached with trepidation, in our clean white lab coats, to the table where our cadaver lay draped with a heavy white sheet. We reverently removed the "shroud".

We were told that this moment would be forever etched into our memory as our first step in becoming a medical doctor, but nothing could prepare us for this unveiling of a cold human body lying on a shiny steel table. We were all young and full of life as "baby doctors," and this was the other end of the spectrum and such a shock. For many of us this was our first glimpse and exposure to immortality and death as a doctor to be. As we gazed upon this scene that most humans would find macabre, most us could not but wonder how old our cadaver was? How did they die? Did they have a family? Were they married? What did they do for work? Did they accomplish all they wanted to do in life? But probably more importantly what made them decide and when did they decide to donate their body to science? The ultimate sacrifice so that we could learn. How would they know how much they would contribute to our learning to become doctors!

At each session in the anatomy lab this body would teach us how the body worked as we flipped through our Gray's Anatomy book matching the pictures to the real thing. The lily-white coats that we started with became more discoloured and permeated with the smell of formaldehyde with each passing session. It would have been nice if the person with a soul who once inhabited this body could have known how much we learned from studying them, subsequently allowing us to save lives, even bringing back some whose bodies were not as cold as theirs back to the warmth of life.

As each session in this anatomy lab passed, most of us became more grateful and appreciative of the individual we would never know "in the flesh" or "in body and soul" for allowing us the privilege of learning from their "bodies of works" and some of us even named our "special person". However, eventually our sessions in the anatomy lab came to an end as our medical studies continued on, but they have never been forgotten. Just like when we witnessed the beginning of life at our first delivery as a baby was born we witnessed the end of life in our cadaver. Both events would forever be with us as memories of becoming a doctor as long as we live.

The lessons learned in the anatomy lab with our cadaver, through dead taught us a lot about life and were part of our passage into becoming a doctor. We would never know how the person whose body we worked on made this ultimate decision to "donate their body to science" allowing us the privilege to learn from them. As well I am sure they probably would have not known the profound effects that it would have on us young doctors. In addition they would have had no sense how many lives they would have contributed to saving over the years of our medical career. In the end because of what we learned from our cadaver, we will be forever grateful for the ultimate decision that they made to donate their bodies to science and to us.

Chapter 6
SEEING THE HUMOUR IN MEDICINE

It has always been said, "Laughter is the Best Medicine". As family physicians we have to see the humour in medicine to get us through the day and to help keep us smiling and positive.

In this chapter I would like to share with you some of the "lighter" medical stories that show you the "Humour in Medicine".

- These stories are as follows:
- You know You're Canadian Eh, When ... (*Stitches*, Vol. 111, June 2001)
- Rules of Paediatrics (unpublished)
- "On the Cover of the CCFP" (CCFP, Letters Vol. 58 March 2012)
- "The Happy GP/Why I Love Being a Family Physician" (*Stitches*, Vol. 128, November 2002)
- "The Doc Whisperer" (*Stitches*, March/April 2006)

- "The Canadian FP EH" (*Stitches*)
- "Stitches in Time/How *Stitches* Saved My Wife" (*Stitches*, Vol. 139, October 2003)
- "Tips to make Your ER Visit Shorter" (*Stitches*, Vol. 149, August 2004)
- Confessions of a Family Doctor (*Edmonton Journal*, January 3, 2001)
- Medical Class Reunion in the New Millennium (unpublished, 2006)

I hope reading these stories will make you laugh and make you a little healthier.

YOU KNOW YOU'RE CANADIAN, EH, WHEN ...

As Canadians, we may have joked about by our neighbours to the south and elsewhere, but at least we have the good sense to be able to laugh at ourselves.

I was inspired to write about this after seeing and hearing the comedians Bowser & Blue from Quebec. They have a skit about what it means to be Canadian, which includes this line," You know you're Canadian, eh, when you're over forty and you play hockey - pause - to win."

With their inspiration, and with Canada Day approaching, I came up with a few of my own. Being Canadian, I'd like to apologize in advance for any hurt feelings.

- You know you're Canadian, eh, when you've had a heart attack and the first question you ask is, "Can I play hockey again?"
- You know you're Canadian, eh, when you wear Wayne Gretzky clothing - and it looks good on you. (Guys, I don't mean Wayne's "home" and "away" jerseys, even though you classify that as a clothing line. I know you wear the black 99 Kings Jersey for formal occasions.)
- You know you're Canadian, eh, when somebody asks you what the alternative national anthem is and you reply, "We Are the Champions/We Will Rock You!" (especially in Edmonton).
- You know you're Canadian, eh, when you put a temporary puck tattoo on your heart, and it doesn't wash off.
- You know you're Canadian, eh, when somebody calls you a loonie, and you think he means you're rich.
- You know you're Canadian, eh, when somebody asks you to give them five, and you hand them a fiver!
- You know you're Canadian, eh, when you still have your Christmas tree up on Valentine's Day, and it's starting to sprout roots in your hardwood floor. (Some of us have ours up all year, and hopefully they're artificial. We Canadians all love that woodsy home living. There are limits, though.)
- You know you're Canadian, eh, when a holiday at a five-star hotel means staying in a tent in the Okanagan with huge satellite dishes on the back of your Chevy pickup and a Coleman stove ready for "room service".

- You know you're Canadian, eh, when your dogs' names are Rocket and Pocket (for Gordie and Bobby).
- You know you're Canadian, eh, when all your jokes are either about hockey or the outdoors.

I invite other *Stitches* readers, even expatriates in "the southern Canada," to send in a few of your own versions of the above.

Oh, I forgot to apologize for the 100th time. I hope I haven't offended Wayne and our other hockey icons. Actually his apparel is comfortable and nice to wear. Oops, there's another Canadian trait. And if this isn't funny to you, then it can't be Canadian as everyone knows all great humour is from Canada, Eh?

Dr. Guy Robert Blais

Previously published in June 2001 *Stitches*. Acknowledgement given to Dr. John Cocker and *Stitches*.

THE RULES OF ENGAGEMENT IN PEDIATRICS (THE SERIOUS AND NON-SERIOUS ONES)

1. Always listen to the mother or the father of the child. You only see the child in a "snapshot" in time. If they state their child is sick, listen to them. They will be right. They know their child. If you don't, you will be making a big mistake. If the caregiver or parent tells you they have tried a medication like penicillin and it did not work last time, respect their word and give them a different one. You will have found common ground with them and usually they will be right. Otherwise, you will have an unhappy parent if they have to come back with their sick child. That is if they do come back. The Doctor does not always know best.

2. Listen to the child or teenager just like I did during my paediatric medical school oral. When I went to take a history and examine the boy he told me that he had been bruising all over and somebody poked him in the hip with a needle to find out what was wrong. I don't think he was told to be so forthcoming but I listened. He helped me figure out what was wrong with him and I passed my paediatric oral because of it (ITP). It may not always be that easy but listen to your patient for the answer of what is wrong with them.

3. Be gentle with your "little patient." It will build trust with them and prevent them from being scared of doctors in the future. There is nothing worse than examining a child who has been traumatized by another caregiver. Even play games with them such as the "Balloon Game," taught to

me by a wise surgeon to examine a child with abdominal pain. By getting the child to "blow their stomach out like a balloon" and then getting them to suck it in like they were making themselves very skinny, you can learn a lot. This way you can get a sense if you are dealing with a serious acute abdominal problem that you need to act on.

4. On a less serious note, if all else fails, make sure you carry stickers in your pockets of the latest super/action heroes, cars, dogs, princesses and Disney characters to reward your "little patients." It always helps them remember you fondly even if you could not figure out what was wrong with them.

These are my rules of engagement in paediatrics. You will not find them in any medical textbook, but they work and come from my experiences with our "little patients." That is part of the art of medicine.

DR. GUY ROBERT BLAIS

ON THE COVER

Guy Robert Blais,, MD CCFP FCFP
Edmonton, Alberta

You know you have made it as a rock band or artist when you appear "On the cover of the *Rolling Stone magazine*". Well, now you know you have arrived as a family physician if you grace the cover of the *Canadian Family Physician*.

This was a brilliant idea. It gives us a chance to "meet" and learn about our family physician colleagues across Canada when we would not otherwise have a chance to do so. This adds to an already excellent medical journal. Please keep up this new tradition, and we all thank you for your hard work in producing *Canadian Family Physician*. Rock on!

Articles from Canadian Family Physician are provided here courtesy of College of Family Physicians of Canada.

Published with their permission.

THE HAPPY GP

by Dr. Guy R. Blais

Becoming a family physician has been much maligned by our specialist colleagues and hasn't been a favourite choice for medical students in recent years, according to the CaRMS Match statistics. So I want to tell you why I like being a family physician so much. It's because:

- What other job allows you to play with kids (stating you're examining them) and get paid for it as well?
- Where else can you hear the latest gossip in your community and not even be part of it?
- How else can you make people faint on command whenever you want, just by proclaiming that you make house calls?
- Who else can find out the latest tips and advice on diets, gardening, car repairs, etc., for free? Just make your patients wait a little longer while they finish their discussions in the waiting room as you eavesdrop around the corner.
- In what other branch of medicine can you have a discussion with a patient about sports, fashion or the weather and actually have it regarded as supportive psychotherapy, with both of you feeling good afterwards?
- How else can you introduce yourself as a body mechanic at a party, where nobody knows you and actually look the part and not be lying about your "trade"? (Note: to be used

when the public is mad at doctors if they take job action during negotiations.)

- Who else can get sympathy for being tired, even enough you've been out late playing hockey with your doctor friends or at a rock concert?
- How else can you go around waking up strangers in the early morning and not get charged with disturbing the peace or get thrown out of the hospital (even if they weren't your patients)?
- Who else can get away with doing phantom "curbside consults" on imaginary patients just to see the specialists' face contort and grimace as he or she waits to hear if this will be the next office patient? (Usually someone who didn't do family medicine before specializing).

There are many other reasons why I love being a family physician so much, but most of all it's because of the fun I have teaching medical students and seeing the looks on their faces when they naively ask to see one of the patient's stool samples - actually a small wooden stool in a film container labelled "stool sample" - and they peer back in disgust at both of us.

I hope I'm promoting the life of a family physician because I've heard, as stated earlier, that medical students aren't choosing this enjoyable "specialty." There's no life like it ... oh, that's the army. I guess using that slogan won't help things. How about, "That's right kids. We're still crazy after all these years."

I'm sure that after the "recruits" read this ode to the family physician there will be a dramatic rise in the numbers applying next year for a family practice residency spot. All you family practice resident program directors need not thank me now, but if my prediction is wrong, then it has to be due to lack of a "humour elective" on your program. You know, curriculum such as the following:

- One week at the Fringe in Edmonton
- A free pass to see the movie, *Patch Adams*
- One week to read *The House of God* and memorize the rules of the House God
- Two weeks to watch medical programs and model yourself after actors such as Howie Mandel as Fiscus, the intern in *St. Elsewhere*
- One week to learn how to be a clown and spread humour

I almost forgot about the last but not necessarily the least important reason why I like being a family physician so much. I get to write about my experiences in family medicine and have them published in a real journal such as *Stitches* and have somebody actually read them when even my family members wouldn't.

Previously published in *Stitches*, November 2002. Acknowledgement given to Dr. John Cocker & *Stitches*

DR. GUY ROBERT BLAIS

TIPS TO MAKING YOUR ER STAY "SHORTER"

As my wife was waiting to be seen in Emergency for an undisclosed illness (you know I had to say that since it is hockey playoff time) we decided to make a list as we waited for the rushed, overworked Emergency Doctor. So we give you:

"The Top Ten Things you can do that will help you get seen in ER quickly and Make Your Stay in Emergency Shorter"

1. Talk to yourself or especially to the invisible person in the chair next to you.
2. Have a list of allergies longer than the list of medications you are on (especially if each allergy comes from a major drug group - so no choices are left).
3. Have a different attending doctor for each medical condition or medication you have and have a different family physician for each hospital in different areas in your city. Make sure to list them even if they are retired or dead; this especially works well at a university based hospital emergency. They are sure enough to find out.
4. Bring in all your medications in a single bottle and ask whether you should take the red one last. Be sure to include the expired ones and forget to bring in the labels, and tell them it is that little blue pill that's missing.
5. State that you feel that Emergency doctors are overpaid and spend too much time on the golf course, or better yet, compliment the Emergency doctor or nurse on their skin colour matching the floor, i.e. ashen grey. Watch as it changes colour to rosy red.

6. Pre-book your Emergency doctor when you check in at the desk (asking to check their tee times - see #5).

7. Bring in your pre-bound medical records and state that is a summary. Be sure to tell them to forward any further records to your lawyer, so he can attach them to your full medical record.

8. Change your "story" numerous times, especially after the student or medical resident has taken it and insist that is not what you told him.

9. Trade your symptoms with fellow ER patients to make things interesting.

And Most Importantly:

10. State you are a close relative of the local Health Minister or Premier.

But in case the top ten don't work, here are a few extra ones to aid in "clear sailing" through the ER (if you know what I mean):

- Be sure to discuss in vivid detail the 3Cs: colour, content and consistency of all fluids from every known body orifice.
- Ask if you come often enough if you can get frequent flyer points or preferred patient status, as you overheard the nurse and doctors talking about frequent flyers.
- Wait for shift change and start all over after you have done all the above. Don't forget to ask for a second opinion from the patient next to you.

My wife and I hope that next time you visit our overcrowded and overworked emergencies that the above tips will be helpful.

Dr. Guy Robert Blais
Elaine Marie Warren-Blais
(co-authors)

THE DOC WHISPERER

Or should it be the patient whisperer? Whatever he is, this family physician has amazing powers!

by Dr. Guy Blais

You've heard of the horse whisperer, and now on TV there's *Ghost Whisperer*. What about the Doc whisperer - or should it be patient whisperer? Don't you feel like that every day? When I talk to patients, they expect me, eerily, to read their thoughts.

"Dr. B I need my prescription renewed."

"Okay, Mrs. S. Is it a pill?"

"Yes. How did you know?"

"Is it circular?"

She replies, "Yes, Dr. B. You can read my mind."

"Now you'll have to think harder. I can't tell if it's a brand name or generic." Dr. B frowns as he concentrates.

"I'm sorry, Dr. B, all I can remember is that it is white."

"Did you take it to control your health?"

"Yes, Dr. B. it is for my thyroid. How did you know?" As Mrs. S smiles as she replies.

"Hmmm ... did I prescribe that to you in the 20th century?"

"Yes, you did, Dr. B. Do you know what it is?"

"Yes, Mrs. S, but I'll have to check to see if it's available in the 21st century. I'll have to consult the special pages of the Blue Book ... Oh, it's coming to me. It's Synthroid," says Dr. B as he flips through his magical Doc whisperer book.

Mrs. S is so impressed that she blurts out, "You're so good, Dr. B! My last doctor said he couldn't remember and told me to have my pharmacist call him."

The next patient is 55-year-old Mrs. V, who wants Dr. B to review her medical history prior to her check-up.

"Have you had any surgery in the past?" he enquires.

"Yes, you remember Dr. B when you were my doctor in 1959."

"Are you sure?"

"Of course."

Dr. B does the math. Despite being a child prodigy, he wasn't practising in 1959, as he would have been two years old. Undaunted, he continues.

"Okay. Was it in a hospital?"

"Yes. See, you remember."

"Mrs. V, did you have pain in your body at that time?

"Yes, I did! How did you know? I had severe pain down here."

Dr. B proudly sings out, "Yes, Mrs. V. You had an appendectomy." (The Doc whisperer calculates she was nine years old and not likely to have had any other surgery at that age.)

Impressed again, Mrs. V replies, "Dr. B, you're so good. It's like you're clairvoyant."

The last patient of the day is Mr. P. Dr. B asks him why he has come in.

Mr. P replies, "The same thing I asked you about three years ago. You remember when I saw you at the Oilers game. But I didn't get a chance to come in like you asked."

As he says this, Dr. B is flipping through his non-existent chart, his spirits dropping. He tries to mind-meld with Mr. P but starts to get a headache, and then it comes to him.

"Yes Mr. P, I remember the beer dripping down your Flames jersey as you held your nachos in your other hand, and of course the Oilers were winning 3-0, right?"

Mr. P beams. "That's correct, Dr. B. You remembered."

The secret was that it was at a hockey game and Dr. B recalls everything about such events. He pretends to be concentrating hard as he replies, "Yes, Mr. P, you came to see me today about your heartburn."

Mr. P is obviously impressed.

"Dr. B, I almost think you should be on one of those shows on TV - you know, like *Dog Whisperer*, or is it *Ghost Whisperer*? I'm sure you could speak to them."

Not a bad idea, Dr. B thinks to himself. It would certainly pay better than this job, and my dog does seem to understand me when I talk Collie to her.

Previously published in *Stitches*, March/April 2006. Acknowledgement given to Dr. John Cocker and *Stitches*.

This month's winning anecdote

(see next page)

Dr. Guy Blais of Edmonton has won a 3M Littman Master Cardiology Stethoscope for this anecdote, which we've chosen as the best in this issue (how could we resist the title?). Send your own funniest medical experience to *Stitches*, 16787 Warden Ave., Newmarket, ON L3Y 4W1 or simon@stitches-magazine.com or fax (905) 853-6565. Each monthly winner is eligible for an annual grand prize.

HOW *STITCHES* SAVED MY WIFE

By Dr. Guy Blais

Edmonton

Late one summer night my wife Elaine was driving back from Saskatchewan, and her back was bothering her badly. So she decided as she came to Lloydminster that she would pull over safely. She inconspicuously came to a complete stop, so she thought, to rest her back.

All of a sudden out of nowhere came a car with red and blue lights carrying a couple of our "country's finest." One of the two Lloydminster RCMPs was male (Elaine later found out he was a rookie) and the other was female.

They asked Elaine what was wrong, and she said she had a sore back and was resting it before continuing her way home to Edmonton. She appeared to be in much pain but told them she was in control of her situation. The two officers were unconvinced, however, and talked it over between themselves whether to let her drive home or make her spend the night in Lloydminster (in the hospital).

Elaine reminded them there was a medical strike in Saskatchewan and said she didn't want to spend many hours in the Emergency Department.

Then a thought came to her. She thought she could help matters by humouring them with a *Stitches* article she'd read about a country doctor, who was flying along the highway at breakneck speed to get to a delivery in a small town at night. Seeing the RCMP pull up beside him as he was going over the posted speed limit, the doctor thought the officer would understand the situation, so he waved his stethoscope at him through the window. But the RCMP smiled back nonchalantly, waving his handcuffs as he pulled the doctor over and wrote him a ticket then gave him a police escort to the delivery.

Well, the RCMP officers laughed together as Elaine finished her tale from *Stitches* of the past. Again, they were lost in thought. Elaine heard the female RCMP say, "Well, it's your call," and then added, "She did tell us that funny joke about the doctor and the handcuffs."

That made his mind up and he let Elaine go on her way, wishing her well and thanking her for the joke.

So that's how *Stitches* saved my wife from an overnight stay in a Lloydminster hospital. (No disrespect to the doctors there but she had a worried husband at home awaiting her arrival.)

Previously published in *Stitches*. Acknowledgement given to Dr. John Cocker and *Stitches*.

CONFESSIONS OF A FAMILY DOCTOR

There seems to be much confusion in these times of changes about what the general public believes a family doctor is in Canada. I hope the following clears that up.

- I am a Doc (at least that's what all my patients call me), I am an FP (family physician) and not a GP (general practitioner).
- My mom and dad were not doctors, but certainly could have been, working such long hours and helping so many people.
- People think that I was given handouts to go to medical school, but the only hands involved were mine working in the oil sands or on the wards for minimal wages.
- I do not golf, but I'd surely like to have the spare time to do so.
- I know and practice the Hippocratic Oath, but I do not remember ever taking it.
- I am not rich, but most people think I am.
- I do not have the dream of owning a Porsche, but I would like to keep my office doors open.
- House calls are made by me, but people think that is an urban legend.
- I treat illness, but I would rather see you well. Rumours state that we don't believe in prevention acts because it is not lucrative; just ask and you'll get the helpful facts.
- I'll do my best to look after my patients, some say, better than I look after myself and my family.

DR. GUY ROBERT BLAIS

- You believe I want privatization of health care as I push for accessibility in the public system I support.
- I am not political, but I'll stand up for what is right (especially for my patients).

Note: A family physician is a doctor with training in a family medicine program, or a practising eligible general practitioner who takes an examination to be certified by the College or Academy of Family Physicians from the country in which they practise.

Previously published in Letters to the Editor in the Edmonton Journal, Wednesday, January 3, 2001.

CLASS OF '81

Outside cover of Yearbook for University
Of Alberta Medical Class 1981. .

HONORARY CLASS PRESIDENT'S MESSAGE

As you near the end of these long undergraduate years may I on behalf of myself, and all your teachers, wish you every success in the years ahead.

I have enjoyed being more closely associated with the Class over these past few months and I look forward to continuing contact with many of you in the years to come.

Medicine is not static - some of you will change its future, some will be changed by it; be prepared to work hard but not to be totally controlled by Medicine. Overall be prepared to be flexible, cheerful and attentive and with this approach very few patients or doctors will ever have any difficulties.

Once again accept all my best wishes for a satisfying life in Medicine.

Yours sincerely,

Dr. John J. Boyd

THE DEAN'S MESSAGE

The reputation of a Medical School depends not so much on the members of its Faculty as on the quality of its graduates.

The Faculty is proud of the Class of '81 and confident that you will bring great credit and honor to the Medical School in the years ahead.

As you now disperse from the classrooms, laboratories and the teaching wards, to seek your careers around the world, our best wishes for happiness and success go with you.

Keep in touch with your classmates, keep alive the many friendships you have made as students. In the years to come there will always be a special bond amongst you as a class and with your Medical School.

God speed.

D.F. Cameron, M.D.
Dean, Faculty of Medicine

First Page in Yearbook.

Guy Blais
Ron Brown
Arla Calman

Bill Campbell
Mike Cassidy
Dean Cave

Raymond Chan
Derek Chu
Nevio Cimolai

Yearbook page with Dr.Guy R.Blais and classmates.

MEDICAL CLASS REUNION IN THE NEW MILLENNIUM

By Dr. Guy R. Blais, MD, CCFP, FCFP

It is hard to believe it's our 25th Medical Class Reunion. Yes, I admit it was the class of 1981. Yes, I graduated in the 20th Century. It's now the New Millennium. We all grew up to be respectable doctors and human beings, well; some of us, but it is time to reminisce.

I remember our Medical School (which will remain anonymous for U's and A's protection) didn't know what to make of us. We seemed too laid back and too carefree for their liking. But they just had the class of 1980, the Davies, McCays, Chernichans, Gormans, Knatkos, Dusts, with no real weak spots in their All Star line-up. KEENERS! Oh, that felt so good to say one more time.

But our class had character and class. Well, as long as you exclude a few, such as an original male classmate who tested his urinary stream by peeing into a beer bottle on a table in Res. Oh, that's okay. He dropped out of our class and subsequently became a Rhodes Scholar and an MD and then a lawyer on the dark side for whoever paid the most (just kidding, Andy).

As well, we had our "John Travolta," who dressed, walked, and wore his hair like him. Not out of imitation but more that this was his style and swagger. He actually went to Rod Stewart concerts.

Dr. "J.T." was also our Dr. Fred Netter. There would be more than one morning when a surprised professor would pull up the sliding chalkboard to start teaching (yes, chalkboard with real chalk - high tech hey?) and find a caricature of one of our classmates. His favourites drawn on more than one occasion were of me as a farmer in my Levi overalls or more classically the "Frankensteinesque" life size one of J.G. This classmate was tall and broad in the shoulders and at times under his gentle demeanour was Frankenstein if he became angry. But he became a legend when one day he entered a ward at the University Hospital to do a consult. The nurse spotted him and started laughing at him with the other nursing staff after their initial shock was over. Dr. Frankenstein turned to see his caricature still pinned to a hospital bulletin board after all these years. The legend lives on.

Then there was Ten Count. You may remember how you practised taking blood on your partner. Well, as soon as she saw the needle she went down to the canvas. Unfortunately, this nickname has followed her all her life (poor Barb).

We had one classmate who bragged he had not started an I.V. throughout his third and fourth year rotations, including surgery. When questioned as to why he avoided doing so, he responded he didn't need to because "I'm going to be a Valium Doctor" He went on to intern in California and became a psychiatrist as far as I know. You might have wondered by that comment and the fact he subsidized his almost non-existent medical school stipend by renting out exotic plants (not the kind you smoke, however). I am not sure what was actually meant by the above statement.

Then there was Ms. Soap Watcher and Ms. Shoe Shopper. I was blessed to do a medical rotation with six female classmates at the old General downtown hospital. They were all hardworking and pleasant except for the two I am about to mention. As medical students (when we worked thirty hours a day and slept only eight hours per night), it was our job to admit patients with medical problems to the ward in the afternoon. On numerous occasions, these two female classmates were nowhere to be found when the work duties were piling up. One day one of the hardworking females was frustrated with them and sleuthed out SG relaxing and watching "General Hospital" in the R wing of the real General Hospital while the others slaved. Sylvia replied that she couldn't miss her soaps. That's okay. She became a radiologist in the "Far East". The other slacker was found later shopping for shoes, and she would only state that there was a shoe sale downtown. I'm not sure what branch of medicine she went into, maybe taxidermy. Is that a sub-specialty?

Can you believe there was one male classmate who was able to condense all his class notes on paper into a duo tang (no computers, remember it was the dark ages, 1981 in the last century) for the full four years of medical school. I think the Smithsonian or Ripley's has asked for it. Maybe he didn't have to write that much down because you know what they say, by the time you finish medical school 50% of what you learn will be wrong and 50% will be correct. You just have to figure out which is which. Sometimes it changes, i.e., Beta Blockers for CHF in use now, contraindicated in 1981. Who knows about Hormone Replacement Therapy? I guess he must have been able to figure out which were the "keepers". Come to think of it, he had a lot of nude drawings in it of anatomy; right?

Then there were the parties I didn't attend enough of and therefore I could make up the stories, but I won't. I'll just tell about a few. There were the Iranian, Protestant, Jewish, Catholic, and other medical students who went out to a nightclub. Sounds like the beginning of our joke. It wasn't. We went to a nightclub to dance, and the bouncer told our Jewish colleague to take off "his hat" that he might have a weapon under it. We tried to teach the "knowledgeable" he-man that this was of religious significance. He couldn't believe it. We told him we were united and would leave if he failed to let him in. Too bad the world of the various faiths and backgrounds were not as agreeable nowadays. As an aside, the nightclub was the same one that threw out "The Eagles" when Don Henley was told by probably by the same bouncer, "I don't care what kind of bird you are. I'm not letting you in."

Next there was the Car Pub Rally. Yes, I know it's not politically correct or appropriate now in the New Millennium, but anyway, "Dr. Travolta" and I were driving in his truck with a full sized skeleton riding shotgun in the cab wearing a cowboy hat. Yes, this medical student actually had a real skeleton that he used to study anatomy. He was also the only infamous medical student who read the pathology text, Robbins, front to back. Note he was one of the keeners in our class. I remember the looks on the people's faces as we drove up to get gas as a Petro station. They couldn't believe their eyes. Astounded or appalled, they asked us if the skeleton was real and the "proud father" replied, "This boy is mine." Can you guess what he went on to become by chance? You could have guessed a pathologist, right!

Then there were our classes other talents. There were the actors, singers and dancers who came out for the Med Show. Who could forget "Battlestar Prophylactica" or "Wizard of Obs.?" Or our gorgeous ladies in the "Flaming Ladies" (He walked in the room ... catchy tune but I wouldn't want to sing it). Then there was the ghoulish Cretin Choir with such hits as "I am so Bloated I'm Passing Some Gas." I would be remiss if I forgot the "Dancing Dentist" (without no brain) - "Wizard of Obs" - get it? At many a medical show he danced disco dressed like a dentist with a six-foot toothbrush to a Donna Summers tune. See what you're missing without a Med Show and political correctness, gone forever – okay. I'll come off my soap box now.

We can't forget our "sports teams". While we can forget our hockey team because I found out (only after facing 100 shots on goal) that they learned to play hockey after Med School and not before. Thanks a lot, Peter & Co. However, our girls' football team, they did us proud. They were feared all over campus in intramural play. They were coached by a couple of our classmates, Dave and Cowboy Brian. One of the stars was a physiotherapist turned medical student (just to be able to play on this team). She played line and attacked and defended viciously, out of keeping with her normal demeanour. They won many games just because of the fear they instilled in their opponents.

I am sure there will be many more incidents that my classmates will "impolitely" remind me of that I forget as we meet for our 25th Medical Class Reunion. It's been some kind of journey, and I would still do it again in this millennium. Some may think I need my head examined, but not by the "Valium Doctor."

So I wish them all the best in the years to come whether in medicine or not.

CONCLUSION OF MEMOIRS OF A CANADIAN HOCKEY DOCTOR

(MEDICINE BY DAY, HOCKEY BY NIGHT)

I had set out to write *MEMOIRS OF A CANADIAN HOCKEY DOCTOR (MEDICINE BY DAY, HOCKEY BY NIGHT)* to give you a glimpse of the multi-faceted life of a Canadian family physician through his writings of his experiences as a family physician and his love of Hockey. This comes from my experiences of living and practising family medicine in the 20th and 21st centuries in Canada.

For over thirty plus years in family medicine, I have seen many changes in medicine, many positive but others I would have not liked changed as outlined in my writings. All we hope for is change that leads to better health care for our patients, our families and ourselves.

From my writings you will get the sense of the tradition and the art of medicine being important to me and how it can't be found in textbooks or on the internet. Also of note just because it is old does not make it wrong or not as good as the new ways. This is where the art of medicine comes into play, allowing the experienced family physician to use all his skills and resources to give the best care to his patients.

However, we must not forget the need for a physician, like other Canadians, to have hobbies such as hockey or writing to make them a well-rounded individual as I try to have come across in my "Memoirs".

So I hope in addition to what I have stated above, that with a bit of humour I have shown that despite the serious side of practising medicine in the past two centuries, we come across humour in medicine daily. Please enjoy the book.

And as always I will be your Canadian hockey doctor playing and practising in Canada. See you in the office or on the ice.

Dr.Guy R. Blais and Elaine Warren-Blais with
Stanley Cup at the Hockey Hall of Fame Toronto,
Ontario (Hockey Hall of Fame Photographer).

CPSIA information can be obtained
at www.ICGtesting.com
Printed in the USA
LVOW06s0619281217
561070LV00026B/689/P